For your reading pleasure

LONDON
UNDERGROUND'S
STRANGEST
TALES

EXTRAORDINARY
BUT TRUE STORIES

A VERY CURIOUS HISTORY

IAIN SPRAGG

BATSFORD

First published in the United Kingdom in 2013 by Portico. This edition first published by
Batsford
10 Southcombe Street
London
W14 0RA

An imprint of Anova Books Company Ltd

ISBN 9781907554971

A CIP catalogue record for this book is available from the British Library.

10 9 8 7 6 5 4 3 2

Printed and bound by Toppan Leefung Printing Ltd, China

This book can be ordered direct from the publisher at
www.anovabooks.com

For your reading pleasure

LONDON
UNDERGROUND'S
STRANGEST
TALES

CONTENTS

INTRODUCTION

The largest subterranean railway in the world, the London Underground has been running relentlessly beneath the streets of the capital since 1863 and the network is now as iconic as Buckingham Palace and Beefeaters, Piccadilly Circus and the Houses of Parliament.

Without the Tube, London would be gridlocked, and each and every year a staggering 1.1 billion commuters and tourists descend on the system to navigate their way across the city, utilising every inch of the network's 249 miles of track and 270 stations.

The mere statistics, however, tell only half the story and since the first train set off on the Metropolitan Railway – the forerunner of the modern Metropolitan Line – back in the mid-nineteenth century, the Underground has become so much more than a prosaic collection of platforms, tracks and carriages. The Tube is now part of London's DNA.

Most passengers, from the seasoned commuter to the Tube novice, experience a curious love-hate relationship with the network. The Underground is the quickest way to get around London but the inevitable service delays can test the patience of even the most phlegmatic passenger. It's frequently the most direct route from A to B, but as all those who have been forced to fight their way into a crowded carriage will know, it's not always the most comfortable journey.

And yet the public's affection for the London Underground shows no signs of abating. It certainly has its faults, but it also has a unique character and it is impossible not to warm its considerable charms.

It undoubtedly boasts a colourful and frequently controversial history. In the pages that follow you will learn of the duplicitous financier behind the Bakerloo Line who took his own life with cyanide, and how a vasectomy brought the Circle Line to an a standstill.

There is the strange tale of the spectral Egyptian Princess believed to haunt the Central Line, and the abandoned station that now regularly appears in Hollywood blockbusters. The curious case of the Tube's own answer to the Eiffel Tower and how a murderous work of fiction nearly ruined the District Line also make a welcome appearance.

My first experience of the Tube was back in 1990. I was 18 years old and en route to Heathrow for that milestone first foreign holiday with friends rather than the family. Lugging my bulging rucksack with me, I remember the looks of thinly disguised disdain from regular commuters on the Piccadilly Line as I clumsily buffeted my way onto their carriage.

I subsequently joined the ranks of the daily travellers when I got my first job in the Big Smoke; my transformation from clueless passenger to veteran commuter began and within months I was instinctively riding the Tube as if I'd been living in London all my life.

Over the years on the network, I have witnessed an impromptu poetry recital by an alarmingly confident drama student, been serenaded by an itinerant calypso quartet and spotted my fair share of celebrities slumming it with the masses.

Of course much has changed on the network since I took my first journey. The introduction of Oyster cards, automatic barriers and even Wi-Fi have dragged the network into the twenty-first century, but the truth is the Underground has constantly evolved ever since the first sub-surface steam-powered trains revolutionised the way Londoners travelled.

The electrification of the network, the introduction of Harry Beck's iconic Tube map and the addition of the Victoria Line in the 1960s have all helped to keep the Tube at the forefront of subterranean travel over the years and, while other networks have tried to imitate it, the London Underground remains the world's definitive subway system.

The Tube has had a profound impact on popular culture over the last 150 years. The network's famous roundel – the ubiquitous red circle and blue rectangle logo – has been copied all over the world, while the legendary 'Mind The Gap' announcement has spawned various novels, a board game, a television show and even an American rock band. It has also been referenced in countless books, songs and films.

This book celebrates the network's long, varied and frequently bizarre history. It answers the burning question of which is the most profitable song for buskers, investigates how many times HM the Queen has actually travelled on the Tube and reveals how a German U-boat landed one Underground grandee in hot water.

After all, the Tube really is much more than just a railway.

BRUNEL, THE WORM AND A TUNNELLING REVOLUTION

1843

Building an underground tunnel in the nineteenth century was a tricky and dangerous business. You painstakingly dug out one section only for it to collapse around your ears leaving you suddenly back to square one with your disgruntled workers demanding danger money, harder hats and regular tea breaks. With biscuits.

It was certainly a problem that vexed Marc Isambard Brunel, the legendary engineer and father of Isambard Kingdom. Brunel senior wanted to drive a tunnel beneath the Thames between Rotherhithe and Limehouse, but all previous attempts to safely navigate below the great river had ended in disaster. What, he mused, was the solution?

Bizarrely, the answer came to him in prison. Banged up for a stretch for failing to pay his debts, Brunel killed a bit of time watching *Teredo navalis* – or a shipworm to me and you – burrowing its way through a piece of wood. He noticed the wily worm avoided being crushed by secreting a slimy trail that quickly hardened as it inched forward to form a tough lining inside the tunnel.

It was Brunel's Eureka moment and, inspired by his uninvited cellmate, he devised a system in which workers would graft away inside a huge protective cast-iron ring. The ring meant the miners could go about their business safe in the knowledge they wouldn't be buried alive – as they made progress, it was shunted forward to the next section. The pristine length of new tunnel behind them was quickly secured with more cast-iron rings and a concrete lining.

In 1825, work on the Thames Tunnel began. Brunel's revolutionary new digging technique worked a treat and after a few false starts, unfortunate floods and various mishaps, the tunnel was finally opened to the public in 1843. Prince Albert was so impressed with Brunel's brilliance that he persuaded the missus to award him a knighthood.

Pedants will of course point out that the Thames Tunnel isn't actually part of the London Underground. That's true, it's now part of the East London Line on the London Overground network, but its successful construction did at least prove it was possible to dig safely beneath London.

They say imitation is the sincerest form of flattery and future generations of engineers were so impressed by Brunel's brilliant idea, they shamelessly copied it, and many of the Underground's early lines were constructed using his protective ring method.

Which all means that had it not been for the industrious shipworm and Brunel's little spell inside, the Underground as we know it might not exist.

PEARSON THE UNPAID PIONEER
1845

It's hard to imagine London without the Underground but the capital could easily have been denied its subterranean transport system had it not been for the determination and drive of a man by the name of Charles Pearson, who was convinced the city needed to dig deep to guard against gridlock.

Ironically, Pearson was not a railway company employee. He didn't make a fortune for his tireless efforts to make the Tube a reality and he didn't even live to see the opening of the Metropolitan Line – the first part of the network – in 1863. But without him, the Underground may never have been built.

A lawyer by trade, Pearson was a radical social reformer. He campaigned against the ban on Jews becoming brokers in the City and for the universal right to vote; he lobbied for judicial reform and was a fierce opponent of capital punishment.

He was also preoccupied with the growing congestion that was blighting London's streets. In 1845 he published a pamphlet calling for the construction of an underground railway through the Fleet Valley to Farringdon and the germ of the idea for the Tube had been born.

Critics dismissed his proposal as fanciful, arguing his trains propelled by compressed air would never work, but Pearson remained undaunted and over the next decade he kept making the case for a subterranean network to keep London on the move.

'The overcrowding of the city is caused first by the natural increase in the population and area of the surrounding district,' he wrote. 'Secondly by the influx of provincial passengers by the great railways North of London and the obstruction experienced in the streets by omnibuses and cabs coming from their distant stations, to bring the provincial travellers to and from the heart of the city.

'I point next to the vast increase of what I may term the migratory population, the population of the city who now oscillate between the country and the city, who leave the City of London every afternoon and return every morning.'

In 1854 he finally started to make headway when a Royal Commission was set up to look at a number of new rail routes for the capital – Pearson once again argued vehemently for his sub-surface solution. Later the same year a private bill to build the Metropolitan Line between Paddington and Farringdon was passed by Parliament and the London Underground came a step closer to fruition.

The line finally opened on 10 January 1863 with much pomp and ceremony but Pearson was not there to see it, dying at his home in Wandsworth in September of the previous year without ever having ridden a train underneath the streets of London.

'Without Pearson's constant advocacy, his gadfly conduct,' reads his entry in the *Oxford Dictionary of National Biography*, 'which he managed to combine with holding high office in the City of London, the Metropolitan Railway, the first of its kind in the world, and the nucleus of London's underground system, could not have come into existence when it did.'

BYE BYE BRITAIN, G'DAY AUSTRALIA!

1857

The Metropolitan Line was the very first piece of what was to become the frighteningly complex London Underground jigsaw, opening to the public in 1863 to usher in a new age of subterranean travel for anyone brave enough to venture into the depths of the network.

The whole project, however, was almost 'derailed' more than a decade earlier when Charles Pearson, the man chiefly responsible for getting the line funded and built, decided to appoint Leopold Redpath as the registrar of his fledgling company and give him access to the petty cash, cheque book and keys to the vault.

Unfortunately, our Leo turned out to be a little light-fingered, and over an eight-year period he managed to embezzle a staggering £250,000 (or £20 million in today's money) from the funds raised to make the Metropolitan Line a reality, depositing his ill-gotten gains in the Union Bank of London.

Pearson and other senior executives at his Great Northern Railway Company were none the wiser until a routine audit of the books in late 1856 rang the alarm bells and they gradually became aware that Redpath was wearing too many Savile Row suits for a man who was supposed to earn only a modest £250 a year.

The Old Bill were called, Leo was arrested for fraud and he was invited to spend a spell as a guest of Her Majesty as he awaited trial.

'He is one of the most notorious delinquents of modern times,' raged an article in the *London Illustrated News* as he awaited his big day in court. 'He is described as a man of good family and prepossessing address and, indeed, it is essential to the success of the systematic swindler that he should possess pleasing manners and a gracious demeanour. Long experience however has shown that some of the blackest crimes have been perpetrated under the mask of nominal respectability.'

The plot thickened when investigations into exactly where all the missing cash had gone revealed that Redpath clearly fancied himself as the Underground's answer to Robin Hood.

'One of the most extraordinary instances of successful swindling, combined with a high moral reputation and a truly benevolent career, is that of Leopold Redpath,' wrote financial journalist David Evans. 'Never was money obtained with more wicked subtlety; never was it spent more charitably. A greater rogue, so far as robbery is concerned, it were difficult to find. Nor a more amiable and polished benefactor to the poor and the friendless. It is certain that he spent in acts of high benevolence much of the money that he gained by robbery. With equal readiness he forged a deed or wrote a cheque for a charitable institution.'

Which was nice but cut absolutely no ice with the judge or jury at his 1857 trial at the Old Bailey, where he was found guilty of fraud and sentenced to transportation to Australia. For life.

The following year, after the Merry Men failed to ride over the hill and save him, Leo was bundled onto a ship from Plymouth to Fremantle in Western Australia along with 279 fellow convicts, never to darken these shores again. Justice had been done and Pearson got his Metropolitan Line project back on track, despite the massive hole in the books.

An interesting footnote to the story is what happened next to Redpath. He spent 10 years toiling away at the Swan River Penal Colony but in 1868 received a pardon, meaning he was technically a free man. The only problem was he couldn't leave Australia, and the next time anything was heard of Leo was 23 years later when his death was recorded at St Vincent's Hospital in Sydney.

His death down under wasn't exactly front-page news back home in Blighty and Redpath's brief cameo in the story of the London Underground was over.

THE LONELY STATION WITH A HEAD FOR HEIGHTS
1867

One of the most curious and overlooked stations on the London Underground surely has to be Mill Hill East, an old, obscure and unloved outpost of the network that vertigo sufferers are well advised to avoid.

Opened in 1867 by the Great Northern Railway (GNR), Mill Hill sticks out all on its own on the High Barnet branch of the Northern Line like the last turkey on the shelves on Christmas Eve. When it was built only a single track connecting it to civilisation was laid, but there were big plans in place to add a second when passenger numbers increased. The opening of the line between Finchley Central and High Barnet put paid to all that, however, and Mill Hill was destined to remain a one-track, shuttle-stop terminus that the other busier, more connected stations laughed about behind its back.

Hapless Mill Hill East does have one tenuous claim to fame, and that's the fact that trains coming in and out of the station have to travel across the impressive Dollis Brook Viaduct, the highest part of the entire London Underground system above ground.

Designed by John Fowler and Walter Brydone, the GNR's chief engineer, this magnificent viaduct comprises 13 arches, each spanning 32 feet to bridge the valley below; at its highest point it stands at an imposing 60 feet tall.

It may not be the most dramatic claim to fame but when your history is as undistinguished and frankly dull as Mill Hill East, any semblance of notoriety is welcome.

THE DOORS TO NOWHERE
1868

Property in London is always in demand but even the most slippery and determined of the capital's estate agents would struggle to sell the two imposing town houses at 23 and 24 Leinster Gardens in Bayswater.

The two properties certainly boast a desirable W2 postcode. They have imposing frontages and fashionable Notting Hill is only a stone's throw away. The only problem is that behind the impressive five-foot-thick façades there are no actual houses, only a rather large hole in the ground that's home to a section of the Circle and District Line.

The fake houses owe their existence to the Underground's first steam engines. The locomotives needed to vent fumes through condensers at regular intervals to keep the tunnels free of smoke, and as the first District Line engineers navigated their way through Bayswater prior to opening in 1868, they realised they needed an 'open' section of track at Leinster Gardens for just this purpose.

The original owners were bought out and the houses demolished, but remaining residents on the street cried foul and demanded the fake façades were built so the new track and plumes of smoke did not adversely affect the look of the neighbourhood.

The Metropolitan District Railway, the company behind the District Line, reluctantly agreed and builders set to work on constructing the new frontages complete with 18 blacked-out windows and two doors (with no letter boxes) that lead absolutely nowhere.

The fake houses, of course, proved irresistible to practical jokers and con artists alike and in the 1930s, a fraudster made a small fortune when he sold tickets for a charity ball at 10 guineas apiece only for the guests to arrive at No. 23 in their finest and discover the party wasn't all they had hoped for.

Since then, local wags have delighted in ordering countless takeaways to the fictitious addresses, laughing themselves stupid as yet another bemused delivery driver unsuccessfully attempts to hand over their culinary orders.

A RIVER RUNS THROUGH IT
1868

The engineers responsible for the first Underground lines and stations faced many challenges but in the early years of the network perhaps none was greater than the problem of keeping commuters at Sloane Square safe and dry.

One of the stations commissioned to serve the Metropolitan District Railway (a.k.a. the District Line) that opened in 1868, Sloane Square happened to stand squarely in the path of the River Westbourne and it didn't take a genius to realise a solution was required to ensure the waterway did not regularly flood the new platforms.

Rising on Hampstead Heath and flowing down through Kilburn, Paddington and Hyde Park before joining the Thames at Chelsea Bridge, the Westbourne isn't exactly a raging torrent but it could not be damned and the engineers were temporarily stumped.

It wasn't practical to build the station above the river because that would result in the building breaking the surface, blocking roads and requiring the demolition of nearby houses and shops. A pumping system to raise and then lower the river above the tracks was dismissed as too expensive and unreliable.

The only solution was for the Westbourne to run *through* Sloane Square, and if you look up from the platform today, you will see the original large, angular iron pipe designed by the engineers that still carries the hidden river safely through the station without spilling a single drop of its watery cargo.

Tragically, Sloane Square was bombed by the Germans during the Blitz in November 1940. The attack claimed the lives of 37 passengers, and injured 79, on a train in the station. It also destroyed the ticket hall, escalators and the glazed roof over the tracks, but miraculously the river-bearing iron pipe survived unscathed.

TRAVELLING LIGHT
1873

People these days are all too ready to complain about draconian modern Health & Safety regulations, but passengers on the first Underground trains would surely have welcomed a little more focus on their wellbeing judging by the risks they had to take to get from A to B.

The early locomotives were steam engines but the carriages they hauled had to be lit to avoid a total blackout, and the only solution was for gas lamps to be installed so businessmen could pore over the *Daily Telegraph* or *Ye Olde Sudoku* on their way to work.

The coal gas to supply the lights was held in tarpaulin bags strapped to the carriage roofs and it remains one of the miracles of the Underground that not once did this combustible cargo go up courtesy of a stray spark from the tracks just a few metres below.

The system was later adapted to a pressurised oil gas set-up, which was only marginally less dangerous than its predecessor.

'The gas bags are weighted on the top and, as the weights descend, an indicator at the side of each box points either to E or F to show how near the india-rubber reservoirs are to being either empty or full,' explained Walter Thornbury in his 1873 book, *Old And New London; A Narrative Of Its History, Its People And Its Places.*

'The jets in the carriages are supplied by means of a gas-pipe in communication with the bags on the roofs and extending from the back of the vehicles themselves, while along the lower part of each portion of the train runs the "main", as it were, by which the bags are replenished from the gasometers established at either end of the line.

'The gasholders are kept charged with supplies from the neighbouring gas-works and are so heavily weighted that the elastic bags along the top of the carriages can be filled (by means of "hydrants" and flexible tubes in connection with the gasholders) in the short space of two or three minutes.

'The light thus afforded to the passengers is so bright as to utterly remove all sense of travelling underground and entirely dissipate that nervousness which the semi-obscurity of ordinary oil-lighted railway carriages gives to the sensitive during their transit through the tunnels on other lines.'

Fortunately passengers were no longer required to dice with death on their daily commute when electric (and less explosive) lighting was introduced in 1890, bringing to an end the Tube's own answer to Russian Roulette.

THE GHOST AND THE NEAR-DEATH EXPERIENCE
1876

There are endless stories of ghosts haunting the London Underground but one of the most 'electrifying' tales of supernatural activity has to be the strange case of Aldgate and the suspicious spectral old lady who made a shocking appearance in the twentieth century.

Built on the site of a plague pit that was the final resting place for an estimated thousand victims of the Bubonic Plague in 1665, Aldgate Station was opened in 1876. Almost as soon as the trains began rolling in and out, the stories of spooky shenanigans began. A popular early tale relates to Tube staff being able to hear ghostly footsteps in the tunnels only for the noise to abruptly and mysteriously stop.

Then an electrician was working at Aldgate one night when he slipped between the tracks, hit the live rail and received a 20,000-volt shock. It could – perhaps *should* – have killed him, but despite being knocked unconscious by his fall, he survived with minor injuries and made a full recovery.

Nothing particularly paranormal perhaps until the accident investigators interviewed the man's colleagues and each of them swore that just before his plunge they had seen the half-transparent ghost of an old woman kneeling down beside the electrician and stroking his hair.

Whether she was the man's guardian angel, somehow saving him from a fatal electrocution, or an Angel of Death, malevolently trying to push him through the gap in the tracks, is a matter of opinion.

THE CIRCLE LINE WARS
1884

The modern London Underground is one big happy family these days, all lovingly managed by Transport for London, but back in its early years the network behaved more like an unruly teenager and there were countless times when the operators of the separate, competing lines just didn't see eye to eye.

One of the most infamous subterranean spats began in 1884 when the Circle Line was finally completed and the Metropolitan and District Lines were connected for the first time in the Tube's history. It should have been a cause for celebration – not to mention reduced journey times – but the Circle Line cheerleaders hadn't reckoned with two rather powerful but extremely petty men who would do their level best to wreck the new development.

The District Line chairman was James Staats Forbes, his counterpart at the Metropolitan Line was Sir Edward William Watkin, and the pair really weren't the best of friends. Perhaps Forbes had once stolen Watkin's lunch money, we just don't know.

The two men briefly put their animosity aside when they agreed a deal to coordinate their trains to make the Circle Line a genuinely circular service, but almost as soon as the ink was dry on the agreement, the problems started that would continue for the next four years.

Watkin got his retaliation in first when he ordered the removal of a number of Forbes' District Line trains from South Kensington, even though they had every right to be there. Forbes hit back by chaining his precious rolling stock to the buffers, only for Watkin to order three of his most powerful locomotives to attempt to break their bondage.

Then the feud moved from the tracks and into the ticket offices along the Circle Line.

After another unseemly bout of name-calling and juvenile finger-pointing, it had been grudgingly agreed that the Metropolitan Line trains would run clockwise and the District Line locomotives anticlockwise on the route.

It seemed a sensible solution – but the two companies refused to sell each other's tickets, meaning an unfortunate commuter might be tricked into a 15-stop journey to get to their destination when they could have got there quicker and cheaper if they'd simply headed in the opposite direction with the 'other' operator.

If only the feuding pair could have resolved their differences, passengers might have been spared years of inconvenience.

SMOKE, BEARDS AND THE WONDER OF ELECTRICITY

1887

Everyone was jolly chuffed when the Metropolitan Line opened in 1863. It was, after all, nothing short of an engineering miracle to dig beneath the streets of London to create the Tube's first tunnels, and as subterranean passengers began whizzing around the capital, the network's designers and architects gave themselves a well-deserved pat on the back.

But there was a cloud on the horizon. Or, more accurately, a fug of smoke in the tunnel. While the Underground's infrastructure was now in place, there was the big problem of the network's steam trains spewing out steam and smoke. Add in carriages full of commuters puffing away happily on pipes and cigarettes and the early Tube was not exactly a clean-air zone.

The owners of the Metropolitan Line initially denied there was an issue. In fact, they even tried to claim an Underground journey was actually good for bronchial complaints, an argument that was somewhat undermined when the company broke with Victorian tradition and allowed its drivers to grow big, bushy beards in the hope their facial fuzz would act as an improvised air filter.

The Underground was getting itself something of a reputation.

'I had my first experience of Hades today and if the real thing is to be like that I shall never again do anything wrong,' wrote American journalist and newspaper editor R.D. Blumenfeld in his diary in 1887 after his own particularly unpleasant introduction to the Tube. 'I got into the Underground railway at Baker Street after leaving Archibald Forbes' house and I wanted to go to Moorgate Street in the City. The compartment in which I sat was filled with passengers who were smoking pipes, as is the British habit, and as the smoke and sulphur from the engine fill the tunnel, all the windows have to be closed.

'The atmosphere was a mixture of sulphur, coal dust and foul fumes from the oil lamp above so that by the time we reached Moorgate Street, I was near dead of asphyxiation and heat. I should think these Underground railways must soon be discontinued for they are a menace to health.'

The finest minds of a generation strove for the answer and a Board Of Trade Committee was convened to investigate possible solutions. Trains pulled by cables and clockwork trams were ideas that never made it further than the drawing board, while the bosses at the Metropolitan Line simply suggested more openings in the tunnels to allow the noxious build-up to escape. The NIMBYs were having none of that though, arguing that even more unannounced emissions would frighten horses, and – horror of horrors – reduce their property prices.

The deadlock was finally broken when a bright spark suggested electrifying the trains was the way forward and, after the problem of getting enough voltage to propel the locomotives up some stubborn slopes was solved, the electrification of the network began in earnest in 1905. Smoke-clogged tunnels quickly became nothing more than a bad memory and commuters could concentrate on complaining about ticket prices, the persistent lack of seats and why the England football team was so poor.

A FRENCH REVOLUTION AT WEMBLEY

1892

The French were inspired to start work on their famed Metro system in Paris after casting envious glances across the Channel at the London Underground. Our Gallic cousins were loath to admit it but they thought the Tube was really rather good and so, during the World Fair in 1900, the Metro was finally opened to Parisians and tourists alike.

But Anglo-Gallic copycat construction in the era was not all one-way traffic and London came close to boasting its very own version of the Eiffel Tower some eight years before Paris unveiled the Metro.

The ambitious project was the brainchild of Sir Edward William Watkin (the man who had the undignified spat with James Forbes), the chairman of the Metropolitan Railway and a man who had a vision for a vast entertainment complex in northwest London served, of course, by his new Wembley Park Station. The centrepiece of the leisure park was to be 'Watkin's Tower', although history now remembers the project as 'Watkin's Folly'.

In 1890 an architectural competition was held to come up with a suitable design for the tower. Ideas for a £1 million plan inspired by the Leaning Tower of Pisa and a building with a spiral railway climbing up the exterior were rejected, as was a design based on a scale model of the Great Pyramid of Giza and Watkin boldly opted for an Eiffel Tower lookalike.

The proposed tower would stand at 358 metres, some 45.8 metres taller than its Parisian counterpart. It was to feature two observation decks, restaurants, theatres, dancing halls and even Turkish baths, and although the great Gustave Eiffel himself declined Watkin's invitation to design his grand plan on the grounds it would be disloyal to the mother country, work on the foundations began in 1892.

The following year Wembley Park Station was opened and in 1896 the park itself was ready for business; sadly, work on the tower was not keeping pace with the rest of the developments and the first visitors to the complex were greeted by the distinctly underwhelming sight of a structure that stood just 47 metres tall.

The bad news just kept coming. Watkin was forced to retire through ill health, engineers discovered the tower's foundations were suffering from subsidence and in 1899 the construction company charged with making Watkin's plan into an imposing reality went into voluntary liquidation.

Watkin joined the choir invisible in 1901 and three years later it was agreed his big idea had definitely been folly and the demolition experts were called to dynamite the whole thing.

The sniggering across the Channel lasted for weeks.

A footnote to this sorry tale came in 1923 when the original Wembley Stadium was built for the British Empire Exhibition on the site of the doomed tower, covering its foundations. When Wembley was rebuilt in 2000, the lowering of the new pitch led builders to uncover the century-old concrete foundations, a poignant reminder of a dream reduced to little more than rubble.

MURDER ON THE DISTRICT LINE
1897

The pen is mightier than the sword and the power of the written word was certainly in evidence on the London Underground at the end of the nineteenth century when William Arthur Dunkerley decided to use the Tube as the setting for a rather macabre tale of revenge and murder.

Writing under his pen name of John Oxenham, Dunkerley's *A Mystery of the Underground* was published in 1897 as a series in the weekly Victorian periodical magazine *To-day* and was so compelling that terrified readers struggled to separate reality from fiction.

The story told of a disgruntled mechanical engineer, known only as The Hood, who bore a grudge against the District Railway Company (based on the Metropolitan District Railway – MDR) and exacted a bloody revenge by travelling on the District Line every Tuesday night, murdering innocent commuters. The series also featured what Dunkerley presented as 'real' newspaper extracts detailing the Hood's gruesome exploits.

The problem was *A Mystery of the Underground* was just too convincing and District Line passenger numbers, particularly on Tuesday nights, plummeted as the fictional body count mounted. MDR complained to Jerome K. Jerome, the editor of *To-day*, that the story was affecting business.

Dunkerley was hauled before his boss and, after a heated exchange of views, he was 'persuaded' to switch his murderous plot to a cruise liner heading down under. The Australian Tourist Board were livid but the MDR, not to mention their anxious passengers, breathed a huge sigh of relief.

William Arthur Dunkerley wrote more than 40 novels in his career before retiring to become the Mayor of Worthing but *A*

Mystery of the Underground remained his most successful short story. In 1997 the bloody tale was revived in a radio play entitled *Death on the District Line*.

'Each Tuesday evening on consecutive weeks the District Line is the location for a brilliant and outrageous murder,' read the PR release. 'Journalist Charles Lester must turn detective or risk becoming the next victim.' Sadly for the passenger commuters on the overcrowded carriages, this time the murderous tale failed to have any negative impact on passenger numbers.

THE FINAL JOURNEY
1898

The London Underground really is a marvellous way of getting around the capital – even if you do happen to be dead and en route to your own funeral. Squeamish passengers, however, tend to frown on sharing a carriage with a corpse, which is why in the long history of the network just two people have made their final journey courtesy of the Tube.

The first was the great Liberal prime minister William Gladstone, who shuffled off this mortal coil in 1898 at the ripe old age of 88. Gladstone spent a lifetime in British politics, serving as prime minister on four separate occasions, and to mark his years of long service he was honoured with a state funeral at Westminster Abbey.

The problem, to borrow a phrase, was getting him to the church on time, so it was decided to transport the coffin on the Underground to Westminster Station. The funeral was certainly a star-studded affair with the Prince of Wales and the Duke of York acting as pallbearers and – after his unusual means of arrival – Gladstone was laid to rest with considerable pomp and ceremony.

Ironically, the great statesman had been one of the guests at the private opening of the Metropolitan Line in 1863, making him one of the very first people to travel on the Tube. Little did he know then that he would be bowing out by the same means of transport.

The second person to be conveyed on the network at the end was Dr Thomas Barnado, the man famous for setting up a series of charitable children's homes. The good doctor died in 1905 aged 60 and spent five days laid out in his coffin in the People's Mission Church in the East End so that thousands of people whose lives he had touched could pay their last respects.

Barnardo, however, had lived much of his life in Barkingside in northeast London and it was there he was to be buried, so a special train was arranged to carry the coffin under the streets of the bustling capital on the Central Line from Liverpool Street to Barkingside Station, which had conveniently opened two years earlier.

At the time of his death, his charity was caring for over 8,500 children in 96 homes and many of them were on hand to see him off. A memorial on top of his final resting place was unveiled in 1908 and, rather thoughtfully, Barnardo had written his own epitaph for it. 'If I had to live over again,' it reads, 'I would do exactly the same thing, only better, I hope, and wiser and with fewer mistakes.'

It remains to be seen whether anyone else will join Gladstone and Barnardo and make use of the Tube on their way to the grave. It may not quite boast the same sense of ceremony as a horse-drawn hearse but it would at least avoid the Congestion Charge.

SHAKE, RATTLE AND ROLL
1900

The early Underground trains were relatively puny machines with about as much power as Nick Clegg in a coalition government, but all that changed in 1900 when the shiny new Central Line was opened and a new breed of bigger, more powerful and altogether more muscular engines were unveiled.

As one of the network's deep lines, the Central needed trains capable of taking the strain so far below the surface and the engineers duly obliged with engines strong enough to take anything the Underground could throw at it.

But big isn't always beautiful and although the new trains did the job they also caused problems, and it wasn't long before the draughtsmen in offices in Cheapside near Bank Station were complaining they could no longer draw straight lines, thanks to the rumble of the testosterone-fuelled trains.

Something had to be done – or at least appear to be done – and a 'Vibration Committee' was set up to look at the problem.

'I beg to ask the President of the Board of Trade whether he will take any steps to secure compliance by the Central London Railway Company with the recommendations of the Committee to inquire into the vibration produced by the working of the traffic on the Central London Railway,' enquired the MP for Paddington South, Sir Thomas George Fardell. 'And whether the Board of Trade will endeavour to prevent the passing of any Railway Bills unless they contain provisions adequately protecting frontagers and others from injury by vibration caused by working of electric traction in Tube railways.'

The President asked in reply whether the draughtsmen couldn't just hold their rulers a bit more tightly and the beefy Central Line trains continued to hurtle through the tunnels.

CENTRAL LINE DÉJÀ-VU
FOR TWAIN
1900

Nineteen hundred was an interesting year. As the long Victorian Era drew ever closer to its inevitable end, it was (as all pedants know) also the final year of the old century, while a surprisingly slim Winston Churchill was elected to Parliament for the very first time, the modern Labour Party was founded and in the United States railwayman Casey Jones became a hero when he died trying to prevent a train crash.

It was also the year of the maiden journey made on the Central Line from Bank to Shepherd's Bush, the first phase of a line that is now 46 miles in length, making it the longest on the network.

There was great fanfare when the line was opened on 27 June 1900 and the guest of honour was none other than the Prince of Wales.

'There was voracious curiosity, astonished satisfaction and solid merit,' the *Daily Mail* breathlessly reported. 'If this kind of thing goes on, London will come to be quite a nice place to travel in. The conductor was all of a quiver of joy and pride. But there was no indecorous exhibition of emotion. Every man was solidly British.'

Every man, that is, except the famous novelist Mark Twain, who was 'most solidly' an American the last time he had looked, yet still found himself on the inaugural Central Line trip.

How the author of *The Adventures of Tom Sawyer* and the critically acclaimed follow-up, *The Adventures of Huckleberry Finn*, ended up 40 feet beneath the streets of London sharing a carriage with royalty is a story as interesting as any of the fiction he wrote.

Twain published *Huckleberry Finn* in 1885 but despite its success and good sales for *Tom Sawyer* before it, he was terrible with money and a series of bad investments forced him to flee the States in 1891 to escape his creditors.

He spent many years travelling the world and lecturing but by 1900 he found himself living in Dollis Hill in northwest London. Despite his financial embarrassment, his reputation preceded him and an invitation for the Central Line party popped through his letterbox.

The twist in the tale comes from a closer look at Twain's early life. Before he became a full-time writer, he served an apprenticeship as a steamboat pilot on the Illinois Central Line back home in America. It's doubtful the organisers of the Underground Central Line bash were aware of the odd connection, but Twain probably had a chuckle to himself as that first train pulled out of Bank Station.

WRIGHT GETS IT ALL WRONG
1904

The early history of the London Underground is littered with colourful and controversial characters and perhaps one of the most notorious was engineer Whitaker Wright, the man who dreamed of constructing a rail link between Waterloo and Baker Street but eventually paid the ultimate price for his grand designs.

In 1897 Wright approached the owners of the fledgling Bakerloo Line and offered to raise the money needed to start work on the new link. They accepted, Wright began trading as the London and Globe Finance Corporation and within weeks he had persuaded investors to part with £700,000 to fund the scheme.

In August 1898 contractors began work and over the next 18 months tunnelling continued at a cost of £650,000.

But behind the scenes all was not well with Wright's other business interests, and in a desperate effort to balance the books and keep himself in caviar and champagne, he issued bonds to raise some cash. When the move failed and was shunned by City investors, Wright illegally began loaning himself other people's money from his other companies.

It was to prove a fatal mistake and in December 1900 the London and Globe Finance Corporation was declared bankrupt. Wright fled to France and excavation work on the Waterloo and Baker Street link ground to a halt.

That might have been the end of the story had it not been for the tenacity of one creditor who had been left out of pocket by Wright. The individual persuaded a judge to issue an arrest warrant for the AWOL engineer and, although he was by now keeping a low profile in New York, Wright was arrested and charged with fraud.

In January 1904 he finally stood trial for his financial misdemeanours at the Royal Courts of Justice. The prosecution was led by Rufus Isaacs, a former broker and City expert, and despite Wright repeatedly insisting they'd got the wrong man, the jury wasn't fooled and he was convicted of fraud and sentenced to seven years' imprisonment.

The real drama however was yet to occur. Proclaiming his innocence and his intention to appeal as he was bundled away, Wright handed his watch to his solicitor (explaining, 'I will need not this where I am going'), reached into his pocket for a capsule of cyanide he had hidden and swallowed it. Wright duly shuffled off this mortal coil, perhaps leaving some investors to consider justice had been done.

The subsequent inquest into his death revealed he had also smuggled a silver-plated revolver into the Royal Courts of Justice, but evidently he had favoured cyanide over a bullet. Wright was buried in the grounds of his sprawling home at Lea Park in Surrey.

'His abilities as a public speaker were turned to good account at shareholders' meetings,' reads his entry in the *Dictionary of National Biography*, 'and inspired confidence in his most disastrous undertakings.'

THE STADIUM THE PICCADILLY LINE BUILT

1905

As the plucky British POWs in the 1963 classic *The Great Escape* discovered, the big problem with digging a tunnel is disposing of all the earth and rubble the excavation creates. It doesn't just disappear magically, you know, and the more you dig, the more unwanted material you generate.

It was a dilemma faced by the early Underground engineers, who were frightfully good at getting their tunnels built but not quite so adept at finding practical uses for the tons of waste their grand plans generated.

That changed in 1905 when a businessman by the name of Gus Mears bought the Stamford Bridge Athletics Ground in southwest London. Mears planned to transform the stadium into one of the greatest football grounds in the country. When nearby Fulham declined to take up residency he decided to form his own team, and Chelsea FC was born.

There was, however, the small matter of the stadium. Stamford Bridge was a modest, ramshackle affair but Mears was desperate to be big and bold, so he approached renowned football architect Archibald Leitch to design him a new ground.

Leitch was happy to oblige for a fee and his plan was to create a vast open bowl around three-quarters of the pitch for terracing, with just one stand with a capacity of 5,000. It was simple and effective, but it needed thousands of tons of building material to create the steep banks that were needed.

Help was at hand in the shape of the nascent Piccadilly Line, which was still under construction and could supply all the cheap rubble and soil Mears and Leitch needed. The deal was done and

Stamford Bridge slowly but surely 'rose to the occasion'.

Mears died in 1912, long before his new team were to become a force in English football, but his family continued to own the club until the early 1980s. Stamford Bridge, which originally boasted a capacity of almost 100,000, certainly lived up to his vision as a top-class venue and was chosen to host the FA Cup final between 1920 and 1922. It staged a rugby union match between Middlesex and the touring All Blacks in 1905 and was also the stadium chosen for a unique baseball clash between the New York Giants and the Chicago White Sox.

The stadium was extensively redeveloped again in the 1990s but this time the builders did not need London Underground's overspill to get the work finished.

THE STATION THAT NEVER WAS
1906

There's an old saying, 'He who fails to plan, plans to fail,' and that was definitely the case when short-sighted American financier Charles Yerkes decided it was high time to extend the Charing Cross, Euston and Hampstead Railway (a.k.a. the Northern Line) between Hampstead and Golders Green.

Despite fierce local opposition to the proposal, Yerkes won the parliamentary permission he needed for his ambitious scheme in 1903 and, once he'd raised the cash to pay for it all, work began on digging the tunnels and the construction of a new station that was a condition of the government's green light.

The key to Yerkes' cunning plan was the farmland that lay above his Northern Line extension, which he planned to develop. The American envisaged street after street of new, gleaming houses – all built by him, of course – with the wealthy residents using his new 'North End' station to commute to work.

And he might have made a success of it had it not been for Henrietta Octavia Weston Barnett, the famous English social reformer, activist and educationalist, who really didn't want Yerkes' ghastly new homes on her patch. Henrietta wasn't short of a few quid and while Yerkes was busying himself with underground excavations, she bought up the land around 'North End' and incorporated it into Hampstead Heath.

It was a strategic *fait accompli*. Yerkes could continue to tunnel until he was blue in the face but without permission to develop above ground, his grand scheme suddenly became a white elephant and in 1906 work on the new station stopped.

Services on the Charing Cross, Euston and Hampstead Railway did begin a year later, but 'North End' had already been bricked up to spare everyone's blushes. The new trains rattled past, oblivious to the abandoned platforms, and while there are 43 other 'ghost' or disused stations on the Underground network, 'North End' holds the dubious distinction of being the only one built that never actually saw active service. Or a single passenger.

It does, however, boast one tenuous claim to fame.

At 221 feet below ground, poor old 'North End' would have been the Tube's deepest station but for Barnett's intervention, rather than a vast underground storage cupboard.

THE TUBE BOSS AND THE
GERMAN U-BOAT
1906

The First World War mercifully left the Underground unscathed. The Luftwaffe was yet to be formed, the Germans did not possess the aerial capability to bomb London and Tube stations did not yet have to shelter thousands of civilians from the menace in the skies.

The conflict did though claim one notable Underground casualty in the shape of Edgar Speyer, an American-born financier and philanthropist from a German family, who in 1906 became the chairman of the Underground Electric Railways Company of London (UERL).

Speyer was a fascinating and generous character. As well as running the Underground from 1906 to 1915, he was the treasurer of Captain Scott's Antarctic expedition, a close friend of Edward Elgar and Claude Debussy, a Privy Counsellor and chairman of the Classical Music Society. In 1906, he was also created a baronet.

How he found the time was a mystery.

His problems started in 1914 when England declared war on Germany. His Teutonic background suddenly didn't make him very popular and he was subjected to a series of vitriolic attacks in the press accusing him of various, unspecified acts of disloyal and traitorous behaviour.

Speyer also happened to own a large country house on the north Norfolk coast and not long after the outbreak of war, hostile crowds began to gather outside his plush pad, jeering at anyone who dared to go in or out. He was even accused of signalling to German submarines at night, although exactly what he was supposed to be signalling was never clear.

'Nothing is harder to bear than a sense of injustice that finds no vent in expression,' Speyer said in a letter to then Prime Minister Herbert Asquith. 'For the last nine months I have kept silence and treated with disdain the charges of disloyalty and suggestions of treachery made against me in the Press and elsewhere.

'But I can keep silence no longer, for these charges and suggestions have now been repeated by public men who have not scrupled to use their position to inflame the overstrained feelings of the people.

'I am not a man who can be driven or drummed by threats or abuse into an attitude of justification. But I consider it due to my honour as a loyal British subject and my personal dignity as a man to retire all my public positions. I therefore write to ask you to accept my resignation as a Privy Councillor and to revoke my baronetcy.'

He also stood down as chairman of UERL and headed back to America, no doubt thoroughly sick of the sight of Britain and its mistrustful natives.

LIGHTS, CAMERA, ACTION!
1907

Everyone wants to be in the movies and the silver-screen dream has come true for Aldwych Station, which today is the London Underground's default location for filming subterranean scenes in Hollywood blockbusters and more modest home-grown productions alike.

Aldwych was opened back in 1907. In the early days, it was the only station on the short Piccadilly Line branch from Holborn and was built on the site of Royal Strand Theatre in Westminster, which had been demolished two years earlier. Little did the engineers know then that the long-term future of the new terminus would lie in the realm of the theatrical rather than in public transport.

During the Second World War it was used to shelter precious artworks from the capital's public galleries and museums, but Aldwych was never particularly popular with paying passengers and by 1993 just 450 people a day were passing through its barriers. It was losing £150,000 a year, London Regional Transport (LRT) faced a bill of £3 million to replace the original lifts and everyone agreed it would be a smart move to forget about the station.

But that was not the end for Aldwych. As a self-contained section of the network closed at weekends and for extended periods during the week, it had already done a spot of moonlighting as a film set before its 1994 closure, and the bosses at LRT decided to maintain the platform and tracks so Aldwych could live on as a full-time movie location. There is even a fully functioning former Northern Line train down there for directors who want to add a bit of authenticity.

Today the London Underground Film Office receives over 200 requests a month to shoot on the network and, although there are other locations, it's Aldwych that hoovers up the lion's share of the work.

Since going full-time, Aldwych has been seen in 2004 British horror *Creep*, 2007 romantic epic *Atonement* and zombie-shocker sequel *28 Weeks Later*. Before it was closed to commuters, it was also used as a backdrop in *Superman IV: The Quest for Peace*, *The Krays* and *Patriot Games*.

Its impressive TV credits include the BBC's *Spooks* and ITV's *Primeval*, while bands like The Prodigy have also used Aldwych's platform and disused tunnels to get that unique Underground feel without the inconvenience of a disorientated tourist walking in front of the camera.

PICK OF THE BUNCH
1907

Many different people helped shape the modern London Underground network that we know and love today, but one of the most colourful and well connected had to be Frank Pick, a solicitor by trade who became one of the network's most influential administrators in the early twentieth century.

At the very least, he was probably the only Tube employee who could honestly claim to have met Churchill, Stalin and Hitler.

Pick was put in charge of the network's marketing and publicity in 1907 when his former boss, Sir George Gibb, was appointed chairman of the new Underground Group, and for the next 30 years he was responsible for every major architectural and aesthetic decision on the system, from the Art Deco design of new stations to the introduction of Harry Beck's iconic Tube map.

His other great achievement was his part in the formation of the London Passenger Transport Board in 1933 with chairman Lord Ashfield, the organisation that finally united the disparate and frequently hostile elements of the network under one roof.

'My job is day-to-day to find answers to a continuous stream of questions about staff, finance, traffic, engineering, publicity, supplies,' Pick explained to his biographer when asked to describe his role as the new board's chief executive. 'In no sense am I an expert. I can obtain advice wherever I want it. I merely have to decide but in deciding I become responsible for my own decisions.'

But it was Pick's incredible encounters with Europe's leaders of the day that really grab the attention.

He met Adolf Hitler at a conference in Berlin in the early 1930s and he also had an audience with Joseph Stalin after his work as a consultant on the construction of the Moscow Metro system. Comrade Stalin was so impressed by Pick's contribution that he awarded the Englishmen the Soviet Union's Honorary Badge of Merit in 1932. Pick accepted the honour but years later found his appetite for gongs diminished, and when he was subsequently offered a knighthood and then a peerage by the government, he turned them down.

Pick met Winston Churchill when he was briefly assigned to the Ministry of Information during the Second World War, but while he and Stalin had apparently got on famously, he and the Prime Minister definitely didn't hit it off.

The pair argued about the ongoing propaganda campaign when Pick insisted it was dishonest to spread lies. Churchill erupted and ordered his secretary to 'never let that impeccable busman darken my door again'. Whether Pick indignantly pointed out he was actually a trainman before showing himself out is not recorded, but his involvement in the war effort had come to an abrupt end.

He died in 1941 but his life is commemorated with a blue plaque outside his home in London's Hampstead Garden Suburb. 'Frank Pick (1878–1941),' it reads. 'Pioneer of good design for London Transport, lived here.'

Churchill may not have agreed but Stalin would surely not have argued with the sentiment.

SELFISH SELFRIDGE'S NAME GAME
1909

Many visitors to London come for a spot of retail therapy and when it comes to shopping there are few more celebrated emporiums than Selfridges on Oxford Street, a Mecca for those eager to splash the cash and melt the plastic.

Opened in 1909, the world-famous department store was the brainchild of American retail magnate Harry Gordon Selfridge, who was something of a visionary when it came to the whole shopping experience. Selfridge wanted a trip to his shop to be fun rather than a chore and, for the first time, the merchandise was put out on display for customers to examine rather than tucked away behind a counter.

As a result, Selfridges was an instant hit, but the man himself wasn't satisfied and the source of his irritation was the nearby Bond Street Station.

To be fair, the station was already doing a sterling job conveying customers to the store, but Selfridge wanted a tunnel built directly linking the station with his premises and he also desperately wanted to rename it 'Selfridges Station'.

His good friend Lord Ashfield was the managing director of the Underground Electric Railway Company at the time and Selfridge lobbied him relentlessly to agree to the new tunnel and the rebranding. The pair had numerous meetings about the idea but – despite rumours that he had promised Ashfield a two-minute trolley dash, loyalty card and an annual Christmas hamper – Bond Street clung on to its original name.

It would of course have set a dangerous precedent and if Ashfield had acquiesced, we might all now be starting our daily commutes at Tesco Express High Barnet, getting off at Specsavers Charing Cross.

THE MYSTERY OF THE ONE-LEGGED ESCALATOR KING
1911

The nature of technological development means that many innovations which today barely warrant a second glance were once new, exciting and even frightening when they were first unleashed on an unsuspecting public.

Escalators are a good example and they caused a considerable stir when two were installed by the Otis Elevator Company of New York at Earl's Court Station back in 1911, linking the Piccadilly Line with the subway that runs below the Circle and District Lines. The new-fangled moving stairs took everyone by surprise and those of a religious persuasion were heard muttering something about the devil's work.

Legend has it that London Transport's tactic to allay passengers' fears about the new contraptions was to employ a one-legged man by the name of Bumper Harris, whose job was to spend all day riding up and down the escalators in a relaxed and jovial manner to (hopefully) reassure any concerned commuters. It was argued that if Bumper could safely negotiate the escalator with his one leg, anyone could – but cynics were quick to ask exactly *how* he'd lost the limb.

Surprisingly little is known about Bumper but the centenary of the Earl's Court escalators in 2011 sparked a search for more information and resulted in this email to the excellent *London-Underground* blog from someone called Aaron.

'Bumper Harris was my great-great-grandfather,' he wrote. 'He was originally from just outside Bristol but moved to London where he went to work on the new Underground. Whilst working some of his friends played a rather unfortunate joke on him and his leg was crushed between two carriages carrying rubble and he lost his leg.

'He was then employed to ride the escalator at Earl's Court. After the Underground, he went on to work on the Severn Tunnel and was in charge of all the drainage systems at Standish Hospital in Gloucestershire, where he retired to make cider, violins and became a watercolourist.'

A diverting story indeed, but the truth is we just don't know whether Bumper was a real person or an urban myth. There is a small model depicting Bumper on his escalator at the Transport Museum's Acton Depot but there is no record at all of him in the London Transport Museum's extensive archives and no mention of him can be found in contemporary newspaper reports.

It is a mystery that is perhaps best left unsolved.

One thing is certain – escalators were a big hit on the Underground. Although nine dresses were torn, one finger pinched and one commuter on crutches fell over in their first week of service at Earl's Court, some 550,000 people travelled up and down them in the first four weeks. London Transport was won over and extended their initial one-month licence period.

Between 1911 and 1915, a total of 22 escalators were installed on the network and today they are as familiar a sight on the network as confused tourists with dangerously oversized rucksacks, harassed office workers and, the most chilling of all, an entire carriage packed with noisy excited children on a school trip.

GAS TRIAL GOES WRONG
1912

Ozone is a naturally occurring gas that was first discovered in 1840, but it was in the 1980s that it really made a name for itself when scientists scared the life out of us by revealing the ozone layer was depleted and we were all in imminent danger of being burned to death by the sun's ultraviolet rays.

Suddenly we all learned to love ozone. But back in the 1910s, Tube commuters were not nearly as keen on the gas when it was deliberately pumped into the network.

The bosses at London Underground were not trying to poison their passengers. Not only is ozone harmless, its oxidising effect also freshens air and kills bacteria, and the idea was to make the network smell altogether fresher and eliminate some of the nasty whiffs that are inevitably created when thousands of people are crammed into confined carriages below the surface.

When the pumping of ozone began in 1912, however, the reaction was not quite as positive as intended. What was envisaged was a fresh sealike scent wafting over the platforms, but passengers were unimpressed by the sharp smell of the ozone, reminiscent of chlorine, and many complained of feeling nauseous whenever the fans were switched on.

Accepting defeat, London Underground quickly abandoned their ozone experiment, but the gas still occurs naturally on the network when the high-voltage electricity used to power the trains reacts with the surrounding air.

No scheme has been suggested to tackle some of the other unwanted gas that permeates carriages today, but a passenger charter in which commuters agree to eschew baked beans would certainly be a good start.

THE FEMALE OF
THE SPECIES
1915

Like many businesses in the early twentieth century, the Underground was not exactly renowned for its pioneering attitude to sexual equality in the workplace. Men ruled the roost and women's involvement with the Tube was almost exclusively limited to making the tea and looking pretty.

All that began to change in 1915 as war raged in Europe and some of London's women were finally entrusted with the day-to-day running of one of the network's stations, paving the way for future generations of female employees.

The historic shift in working practices came with the official opening of Maida Vale Station in a now-affluent area of northwest London in June 1915, part of an extension of the Bakerloo Line from Paddington to Queen's Park. The station required two ticket collectors, two porters, two booking clerks and two relief ticket collectors to run smoothly, but with an increasing number of men abroad fighting in the Great War, radical measures were required.

The solution of course was to recruit female staff and – resplendent in their uniforms of black leggings, blue tunics and broad-brimmed felt hats – the eight pioneering women took up their new jobs as Maida Vale opened its doors to passengers for the first time.

An all-female station was certainly revolutionary but even more surprising was the decision by the line's owners – the Underground Electric Railways Company of London – to pay its new staff the same salary as their male counterparts a full 60 years before the implementation of the Equal Pay Act.

That Maida Vale was still technically run by an off-site, male stationmaster was a mere detail.

The following year the London General Omnibus Company (LGOC) also began to recruit women; in all it was estimated that 5,551 women had been employed on the Underground during the war years.

One of the beneficiaries of the Maida Vale revolution was Hannah Dadds, who made history in 1978 when she became the first ever female Tube driver on the Underground.

Born in Forest Gate in 1941, Hannah initially worked as a ticket collector and then guard on the network and ignored the Neanderthals and nay-sayers when she decided to enrol at 'driver school'.

It took her seven weeks to learn the ropes but on 5 October 1978 she qualified, despite the instructors' thinly disguised hostility to her presence. 'I was asked more questions than any man,' she recalled. 'There was five of us from the District Line together in the classroom – four men and me – and I was definitely asked more questions. Even if a question wasn't directed at me to start with, the trainer would come back and say, "Do you agree with that, Mrs Dadds?"'

Hannah drove without incident or accident until she retired at the age of 53. She moved to Spain but was back in Britain in 2004 when she was invited to Buckingham Palace to meet the Queen as part of the Women of Achievement Awards.

She passed away in 2011 at the age of 70 but her legacy lives on in the shape of the ever-increasing number of female drivers on the network. In 1990 just 30 of the Underground's 2,500 drivers were women; by 2001 the number had risen to 167.

That rise was in no small part thanks to a series of adverts calling for female recruits run by London Underground in between articles about orgasms and Jimmy Choo in *Cosmopolitan* magazine, a campaign that proved a resounding success.

'The Tube recorded a peak-time performance last month, largely because of the impact of women drivers,' reported *The Times* in 2002. 'They have endured taunts from male colleagues and abuse from passengers but the army of women drivers recruited by

London Underground have proved that they are better than men at making Tube trains run on time. Managers believe that their influence has helped to end a culture of absenteeism and militancy in the workplace.'

HOLDEN, HITLER AND
THE NEW-LOOK TUBE
1923

Graduating from designing graveyards to become one of the most influential architects in the history of the London Underground may not be the most traditional of career paths but it is nonetheless the unusual story of Charles Henry Holden, the man responsible for 33 of the network's 270 stations from Acton Town to Wood Green, Arnos Grove to Westminster.

Born in Bolton in 1875, Holden studied at the Manchester School of Art but at the outbreak of the First World War became an army lieutenant and served with the Directorate of Graves and Registration and Enquiries, planning new cemeteries in France and expanding the existing ones. The following year he transferred to the Imperial War Graves Commission as a major and between 1918 and 1928 he helped design 69 new cemeteries.

It was after the end of hostilities when he met Frank Pick, by now the general manager of the UERL, that Holden really made his architectural mark.

Pick initially commissioned Holden to design a façade for a side entrance at Westminster Station in 1923 and was so impressed by the work that the following year he asked him to draw up plans for seven gleaming new stations for the extension of the City and South London Railway, or the Northern Line to you and me.

During the rest of the 1920s and 1930s, Holden was top dog, the man to whom London Underground turned to create the new termini they needed as the network expanded. In 1930, he made a tour of Germany, the Netherlands, Denmark and Sweden to see the latest developments in modern architecture; the Continental influence – the cylinders, curves and rectangles – can clearly be seen in his work on stations on the Piccadilly Line extension.

His last Tube work was for three new stations for the Central Line extension (work delayed by the Second World War), but Holden was no one-trick pony and worked on many other projects across London including Senate House, a design which earned him a rather unpleasant claim to fame.

An Art Deco building commissioned by the University of London and built between 1932 and 1937, Senate House is said to have inspired George Orwell's Ministry of Information in his classic *Nineteen Eighty-Four*, but it was the admiration of a certain Adolf Hitler that Holden could really have done without.

The Führer was apparently a big fan of Senate House. He ordered the Luftwaffe to give the building a wide berth during the Blitz, or else, and he also planned to use it as his London HQ after a successful invasion of Britain.

While Hitler's plans didn't go quite according to plan, Holden was said to be far from impressed when the identity of his biggest fan was revealed.

BABIES ON BOARD
1924

Offering your seat to a pregnant woman on the Underground is an act fraught with danger and what is often intended as an act of chivalry can quickly result in acute social embarrassment when you realise the lady in question is probably on her way to WeightWatchers rather than with child.

The danger for pregnant women, however, is actually giving birth while on the Tube, and the first recorded incident of a new life arriving on the network was in May 1924 at the Elephant & Castle Station when a certain Marie Cordery just couldn't hold on.

Details of the happy if unusual occasion are sketchy. The newspapers of the day reported the baby girl had been named Thelma Ursula Beatrice Eleanor, which was a nice story because her initials spelled out 'Tube'. It wasn't until 2000 when she was traced for a television interview that it emerged she was in fact called Mary Ashfield Eleanor and took her second name from her godfather Lord Ashfield, who was the chairman of the London Passenger Transport Board at the time of her impromptu delivery.

The second recorded birth on the London Underground came 84 years later in 2008 when Julia Kowalska didn't quite make it to the hospital in time and went into labour at Kingsbury Station on the Jubilee Line.

'At 9 p.m. the station supervisor received a message from the control room that a woman on a northbound train was complaining of stomach pains,' explained a Transport for London spokesman. 'A few minutes later the supervisor went to the platform and found the pregnant woman having contractions and called an ambulance.

'The woman, accompanied by her sister, was wrapped in a foil blanket to keep warm and taken to the supervisor's office where the ambulance crew delivered a healthy baby girl.'

Two births and two girls, but a baby boy finally made an appearance in May 2009 when 32-year-old Michelle Jenkins was travelling on the Jubilee Line and realised the puddle in front of her was her waters breaking rather than a stray bottle of Evian. She was rushed to the office at London Bridge Station and gave birth with the usual gnashing and wailing but thankfully no complications.

There is another story of a birth on the network in 1944, but whether American talkshow host Jerry Springer really did come into this world on the platform of East Finchley Station is a moot point.

'I was born during the Second World War [in London] and women in their ninth month would spend the nights in the subway stations because those were the shelters,' Springer once claimed in an interview. 'Hitler was bombing every night. So I was born at 11.45 at night and every time I hear a train go by I still jump.'

The only problem with the story is the fact that East Finchley is an overground station. It certainly wouldn't have provided much protection from the Luftwaffe during the Blitz and was never an official wartime shelter.

It would have made far more sense had Mrs Springer gone into labour just up the Northern Line at Highgate, a nice, deep station that offered plenty of cover from Hitler's bombs. Perhaps she got confused as the air-raid sirens sounded or maybe little Jerry simply didn't listen properly when his mum told him the story of his unusual birth.

THE TEENAGER IN THE DRIVER'S CAB

1924

London Underground drivers usually have to undergo years of meticulous training before they are finally let loose on a real train, but regulations on the network were obviously a little more relaxed back in the 1920s judging by the strange story of Anthony Bull.

A public transport enthusiast from an early age, Bull just happened to be the third son of the well-known MP for Hampstead and when the new section of the Northern Line between Highgate and Moorgate was opened in 1924, Daddy pulled a few strings and the 16-year-old Anthony was invited to drive the first train down the tracks via the Camden Town loops.

The *Daily Mail* described him as 'this lucky London boy' while his passengers perhaps opted for more descriptive four-letter words when they discovered an unqualified teenager had been allowed to drive their train.

To be fair to Bull, his experience was wasted on him and after graduating from Cambridge University in 1929, he returned to the scene of the crime and joined the London Underground Company as a clerk on an annual salary of £120.

He quickly rose through the ranks, becoming assistant secretary to Lord Ashfield, the chairman of the London Passenger Transport Board (LTB), and then assistant to Frank Pick, the vice-chairman. By 1965 he had become vice-chairman of the LTB in his own right and played a major role in the planning and construction of the Victoria Line.

It was at the opening of the new line in 1968 that Bull met the Queen and Her Majesty decided to have a quick chat with the Underground *grand fromage*. 'You must be glad now that it is open,' she politely asked. 'Yes,' said Bull as he bowed, 'but what pleases me most is that it has opened on time and within the cost estimate.' To which, quick as a flash, Liz replied, 'That makes a change.'

A frustrated comedian obviously, Her Majesty.

PARKING AT MORDEN
FAILS TO IMPRESS
1926

Driving to an Underground station and parking your car before jumping on a train is either a prohibitively expensive or physically impossible task in London, depending on where you live. Tube stations either charge a small fortune for the privilege of parking or there simply isn't a car park in sight.

It wasn't always meant to be like this and in the embryonic days of the network, there were grand plans for the Tube and cars to enjoy a far more symbiotic relationship.

A shining example of such a tie-up was Morden, the southern extreme of the Northern Line, which was opened in 1926 as a new extension of the City & South London Railway from Clapham Common.

Located in a then rural area, the idea was to encourage commuters to bring their vehicles to the station before taking the train; to incentivise them, there were 500 parking spaces for season-ticket holders. There were also petrol pumps, workshop facilities and mechanics on site to lovingly tend to their prized motors.

The innovative approach to marrying the two forms of transport was the first of its kind in the country, but problems were just around the corner and as London's urban sprawl spread inexorably outwards to swallow up places like Morden, property values shot up. Landowners and businessmen realised there was far more money to be made from building houses than car parks and garages and the copycat stations, modelling themselves on Morden, failed to materialise.

The legacy of Morden's failure can still be felt today as Londoners are forced to take out second mortgages merely to pay for parking in the same postcode as their nearest Tube.

HARRY POTTER, HARRY BECK AND THE TUBE MAP

1933

From Tottenham Hale to Timbuktu and Fulham Broadway to Fiji, the iconic map of the London Underground is as famous as the network itself and every year millions of bemused passengers rely on its clean, coloured lines to navigate their way through the maze that is the Tube.

It's so famous, in fact, that it even gets a mention in the series of Harry Potter books. 'Scars can come in handy,' says Hogwarts' headmaster Dumbledore in *Harry Potter and the Philosopher's Stone*. 'I have one myself above my left knee that is a perfect map of the London Underground.'

The real map was the brainchild of Harry Beck, an engineering draughtsman from Finchley who worked for the London Underground Signals Office but spent his spare time drawing up transport system diagrams and whose passion to simplify the Tube map resulted in today's classic design.

The early, pre-Beck Tube maps were a real mess. Although they were geographically accurate, reflecting where the various lines ran under the capital and how far the journey was between each station, the end result looked more like someone had inadvertently dropped a can of Heinz Spaghetti on a piece of A4 paper, and commuters were often none the wiser how to complete their journey.

Beck had a better idea and reasoned that what passengers really wanted was a nice, simple design that clearly showed how to get from A to B. He also argued that since commuters were pretty much stuck in their carriages between stations, it really didn't matter how far it was between stops.

'Looking at an old map of the Underground railways,' he said, 'it occurred to me that it might be possible to tidy it up by straightening the lines, experimenting with diagonals and evening out the distance between stations.'

The result was his easy-to-use, virtually idiot-proof Tube map; he submitted his radical new design in 1931. London Underground were initially sceptical and it wasn't until the following year that they finally agreed to a trial production of 500 copies to test the water. Beck's map was an instant hit and in 1933 700,000 copies were issued. A month later, the order went out for an ever larger reprint.

'The genius of Beck was that he realised that the exact geographical or topographical course of the line is not necessarily essential to the Underground passenger,' said Claire Dobbin, senior curator at the London Transport Museum in 2012, during an exhibition to celebrate Beck's creation.

'The London Tube map is one of the most widely recognised maps in the world. It has inspired artists and cartographers, been the subject of academic debate and has been printed on more products than Beck could have thought imaginable.

'It has certainly become part of popular visual culture and even a symbol of London itself, but none of these things provide a more appropriate measure of the diagrammatic map's success than the fact that it is still in use, fulfilling the function it set out to do 80 years ago.'

Over the years other people have tweaked Beck's original design but the modern map remains essentially his baby and in 2006 viewers of BBC's *Culture Show* and visitors to London's Design Museum voted it the second greatest British design of the twentieth century behind Concorde. In 2009 the map featured on a Royal Mail stamp, and one of his original maps is still preserved on the southbound platform at Finchley Central Station.

Beck, who died in 1974, never found fame or fortune as a result of his work. He was paid a miserly five guineas – around £230 in today's money – by London Underground for his design and it is only in the last 20 years that he has received the posthumous recognition his efforts surely deserved.

THE CURSE OF THE EGYPTIAN PRINCESS
1933

The ancient Egyptians were an innovative bunch. They invented the pyramids, eye make-up, paper, calendars and even toothpaste, but arguably their most enduring legacy has been their fondness for mummifying their dead and the slew of ghost stories that have sprung up as a result.

The London Underground, of course, has its own spooky Egyptian legend.

It centres on the long since blocked-up British Museum Station which, as the name suggests, was close to the British Museum. The station was opened in 1900 by the Central Railway Company and, soon after, reports of anguished screams in the tunnels began to emerge.

The popular theory was that the blood-curdling noise that travelled all the way to neighbouring stations was being made by the ghost of the daughter of Egyptian pharaoh Amen-Ra. Her coffin lid – or 'mummy board – was on display at the nearby museum and erroneously dubbed the 'Unlucky Mummy'; the artefact had already been linked to a series of mysterious deaths and disasters.

The story of the wailing Egyptian princess spread like wildfire and although the British Museum Station closed in 1933, the rumours persisted and *The Times* offered a reward to anyone willing to spend a whole night on the deserted platform. No one was brave enough to take on the challenge.

Things got even stranger in 1935 when Gaumont International released a film called *Bulldog Jack*. The movie used the Amen-Ra curse as its central plot device and climaxed with a dramatic chase through a secret tunnel that connected the British Museum's

Egyptian Room with the station. On the same night as the film premiered in London, two women were said to have disappeared from nearby Holborn; the next day, supposedly, two unexplained marks had appeared on the walls of the station.

Ever since the release of the film, London Underground has adamantly denied the existence of any clandestine tunnel between the station and the museum ... but they would say that, wouldn't they?

ANYONE FOR CRICKET?
1939

The English love of cricket is world famous and legend has it that part of the modern Bakerloo Line owes its existence to our national obsession with the thwack of leather on willow, cream teas and unfathomable fielding positions.

The story focuses on Lord's Cricket Ground, which was originally served by the imaginatively named Lord's Station on the Metropolitan Line. By the mid-1930s, however, the strain on the line between Baker Street and Finchley Road was beginning to take its toll and the obvious solution seemed to be extending the Bakerloo Line northwards to relieve the pressure.

The expensive scheme hung in the balance but rumour has it the proposal finally got the green light when a number of wealthy businessmen realised the extension could help them get to the home of cricket with the minimum of fuss.

And so it (allegedly) came to pass that the Bakerloo extension was made a reality and in 1939 the new St John's Wood Station – a mere straight drive from Lord's – was opened, while dear old Lord's Station was deemed surplus to requirements and consigned to the dustbin of history.

The fact that any self-respecting millionaire would only arrive at the famous ground in a chauffeur-driven Rolls these days is neither here nor there.

UNDERGROUND GETS ROYAL SEAL OF APPROVAL

1939

The Queen has a fleet of classic cars, priceless horse-drawn carriages and even private helicopters at her disposal whenever she needs to get about town, which probably explains why Her Majesty HRH has only ever jumped on an Underground train three times in her life.

Her first experience of the Tube came in 1939 when HRH was just 13 years old and yet to ascend to the throne. She was joined on her journey by sister Margaret, nanny Marion Crawford and a rather conspicuous minder who failed to grasp the whole concept of covert mission.

'One day, as we passed Hyde Park Corner, there were people streaming out of the Underground station,' Crawford remembered in her book *The Little Princesses: The Story of the Queen's Childhood by her Nanny*, which was published in 1950 and caused quite a stir in royal circles. 'Lilibet said wistfully, "Oh dear, what fun it must be to ride in those trains." I thought why not?

'The Duke [the future King George VI] agreed we could go, provided we were accompanied by the house detective. As part of the fun, the girls bought their tickets themselves. The whole business was as solemn as an investiture. They took an immense time getting the money out of their little embroidered purses and then collecting their change.

'On the escalator, Margaret's hand tightened on mine and she swallowed apprehensively. Once we'd boarded a train, both girls sat there, wide-eyed and enchanted until they became aware of a small commotion.

'Their detective, who was standing at the far end of the carriage, looked so very obvious that people were looking round to see what he was detecting. Mercifully, we arrived at Tottenham Court Road and got out before anyone had spotted the Princesses.'

The Queen's next foray below the surface was not until 1968, when the opening ceremony for the Victoria Line was held, the first time a reigning monarch had travelled on the Tube.

Having fed the corgis and locked away the family silver, Her Majesty arrived at Victoria and, after unveiling a commemorative plaque on the station concourse, she boarded a train heading for Green Park. Rather embarrassingly, the organisers made Liz buy a ticket for her journey in a blatant breach of protocol and one of the rare times during her reign she has ever actually needed cash.

The train she rode was quickly dubbed 'The Royal Train' and is now housed for prosperity at the TfL depot at Acton.

Her Majesty's most recent journey was in 1977 when she showed her familiar face at the opening of the Piccadilly Line extension and, because she'd been a very good girl, she got to ride in the driver's cab for the trip from Hatton Cross to Heathrow.

Luckily this time they didn't make the faux pas of asking HRH to pay for her trip.

UNDERGROUND ENTERTAINMENT
AS THE BOMBS FELL
1940

When the Luftwaffe began bombing the capital in September 1940, Londoners realised that hiding under the kitchen table wasn't going to provide enough protection from the falling bombs and all eyes quickly turned to the Underground's deep-level stations as the perfect place to shelter from the Blitz.

The problem was that the government, safe in their purpose-made bunkers in Whitehall, decided the Tube was for passengers only, and an uneasy stand-off ensued despite the people's quite reasonable contention that it was bloody dangerous up on the surface.

The situation reached a head on the evening of 8 September 1940 when a large, frightened crowd gathered outside Liverpool Street Station and demanded to come in. A line of Underground employees and Home Guard blocked their way but the mob weren't willing to be blown to smithereens, whatever Churchill said, and forced their way through, starting the famed subterranean exodus of Londoners onto the Underground during the war.

By the middle of September, an estimated 150,000 people were sleeping on the network each night and the impromptu shelters rapidly adapted to their new role with beds, medical and sanitation facilities all introduced to make life that little more bearable.

But boredom was also a factor during the long nights of bombing and the Tube quickly became an unlikely hub of entertainment as Londoners avoided the explosions above them. Fifty-two stations suddenly acquired libraries, and concert parties, informal dances and sing-songs were a common occurrence. An amateur drama group toured the packed stations with a production of Chekhov's

The Bear, there was even an inter-shelter darts league, and makeshift bars were also set up to take the edge off things.

By May 1941, the worse of the Blitz was over and Londoners emerged from the tunnels to assess the damage. Some were shocked by the scenes of devastation while others were simply grateful they would no longer have to spend their evenings listening to George Formby – a regular visitor to Aldwych Station – and his bloody banjolele!

THE FORGOTTEN FACTORY
THE GERMANS NEVER FOUND
1942

The Underground's heroic role as a shelter for thousands of London's terrified residents during the Blitz is well documented, but a few miles east from the centre of the city, the Tube was playing a different and altogether more secret role as German bombs continued to fall.

The location was a five-mile stretch of temporarily disused track that ran through Wanstead, Redbridge and Gant's Hill Stations, and the secret it was hiding was a factory supplying radios, telephones, and shell and bomb cases for the Allied war effort.

The factory was operated by electronics firm Plessey, who needed somewhere safe to go about their vital business after the infuriatingly accurate Luftwaffe had destroyed their original building in Ilford in late 1940. They turned to the Air Ministry and London Transport and after spending £500,000 to convert the Tube tunnels, the factory was completed in March 1942.

To describe the new facility as big would be an understatement. In fact, it was so cavernous that 2,000 people could beaver away at the machines at the same time and there was a grand total of 300,000 square feet of space. It was so huge that Plessey's foremen were issued with bicycles just to get from one end of the place to the other.

And in the four years the factory continued to churn out supplies, it was never hit in a bombing raid.

'The Luftwaffe never got to know about us,' recalled Dennis Barron, who worked at the factory as a stores manager. 'We were safe. Riding my bike to work from Dagenham during an air raid was the dangerous part. I once ran like hell when a plane zoomed down and the machine guns let rip.

'Getting to the loo in a hurry was the only dodgy thing I can remember about working in the tunnels,' he added. 'Sometimes it could mean a mile's sprint.

'I worked from 7 a.m. until 6 p.m., five days a week and half-day Saturday. And for that I got £1.50 a week, which was quite a lot of money for a boy of my age in those days.

'Of course, these hours meant I didn't get to see much daylight for half the year, apart from a few minutes at lunchtime sometimes when I nipped out for fish and chips as a change to the canteen's sandwiches.'

After the war, the factory was closed down when the Central Line was brought slowly back to life and commuters rather than plucky subterranean workers once again became the norm at Wanstead, Redbridge and Gant's Hill. An estimated 8 million shell casings were manufactured between 1942 and 1946 before this one particular stretch of Underground got back to its day job.

'During these four years, the works operated day and night and the number of workers at the peak period was about 4,000,' ran an article in the *London Illustrated News* in 1947. 'The stations were used for offices, stores and first aid. Many millions of components were produced, among them being aircraft pumps, cartridge engine starters and breeches, aircraft wiring components, radio components, magnetos, field telephones, gear-cutting tools, gear levers and other components for armoured cars, shell fuses and so forth.'

The factory, of course, brought a whole new meaning to the phrase 'underground resistance'.

IT'S A DIRTY JOB BUT
SOMEONE'S GOT TO DO IT
1947

To those with a working knowledge of the adult entertainment industry, a fluffer is someone charged with ensuring the male stars are 'ready for action' when the cameras roll. For those with their minds not in the gutter, a fluffer is someone whose job it is to clean the Underground's tracks while everyone else is safely tucked up in bed.

The problem with the Underground is the trains tend to suck in dust and other detritus into the network's tunnels as they career along. The debris has to be cleared away because it's a serious fire hazard should a stray spark from the carriage wheels land in the wrong place. And so for decades teams of fluffers have been despatched down the Tube at night to sweep up the mess once the last train has departed and the electricity has been switched off.

For years commuters were blissfully unaware of the fluffers' vital contribution to the safe running of the network. Then in 1947 British Pathé finally captured them in action, complete with carbide lamps, long brushes, dustbins and scraping tools. Fluffers returned to our screens in 1989 when Molly Dineen made a TV documentary entitled *Heart of the Angel*, capturing 48 hours in the life of Angel Station.

The boffins at Transport for London have spent years trying to come up with a mechanical solution to the problem and while a cleaning train known affectionately as the 'Big Yellow Duster' does now patrol the Tube's tunnels at night, picking up all manner of debris, fluffers are still deployed – you can't quite beat the human touch.

Fluffers were traditionally female and the job was dirty and monotonous, forcing the subterranean crews of cleaners to make their own entertainment whenever and wherever possible.

'I took home-made food into work on Friday nights and my friend Bernie took in whisky,' recalled Evelyn Roberts, who worked as a fluffer in the 1950s and 60s after coming to the UK from Barbados. 'We would have a little party and then work through the night. One weekend my friend Mertle had too much whisky and was ill, she was sick. She carried on working, not realising she had lost her teeth. It was my other friend Rosie who found them on the platform in the morning. She worked the shift without her teeth, she was a bit tipsy.'

AIN'T NO SUNSHINE ANY MORE
1948

The arrival of the first emigrants from Jamaica on the *SS Empire Windrush* is a famous part of British history, but the 492 brave souls who boarded the boat in Kingston in 1948 probably had no idea they'd be forced to sleep on the Underground when they finally arrived in rain-soaked Blighty.

The Jamaicans came to post-war Britain after reading an advert in the *Daily Gleaner* offering transport to the UK at a knockdown rate. Jobs, housing and relentless drizzle were all on offer and on 22 June 1948, the *Windrush* steamed up the Thames to Tilbury Docks with its expectant passengers.

After realising it had been a big mistake to pack their sun hats and shorts, they disembarked and those who had already made arrangements headed off to begin their new lives.

'Some of the Jamaicans who arrived in Britain yesterday in the *Empire Windrush* wore expensive suits,' observed the fashion section of the *Daily Mirror*. 'There were even emigrants wearing zoot-style suits, very long-waisted jacket, big padded shoulders, slit pockets and peg-top trousers costing 15 to 28 pounds. There were flash ties and white-and-tan shoes.'

The Colonial Office and Ministry of Labour, however, hadn't really given much thought to where the rest of the new arrivals would stay and hastily decided the old deep air-raid shelter under Clapham Common Station would suffice as a temporary home for the remaining 230 newcomers.

The shelters were made of two, 1,200ft-long tunnels. A reception tent was set up at the top of the entrance shaft and after 'checking in', the Jamaicans were each given a linen sheet and grey blanket, allocated a bunk and taken down to their new home in a rickety lift.

'It was the bowels of south London,' said one of the unlucky new residents. 'We curiously eyed the network of poorly lit, clammy, musty tunnels that had been offered as residence. It was primitive and unwelcoming, like a sparsely furnished rabbit's warren. But in a strange new land, there were few alternatives.'

Ruefully remembering the Caribbean sun, the Jamaicans quickly took to relaxing on the Common to escape the claustrophobia of the tunnels and as soon as they could, they found jobs and got the hell out of there.

CATTLE REPLACE COMMUTERS
1960

Passengers are the London Underground's *raison d'être*. Without them, the network would simply be a cavernous white elephant (and the narrow roads of the capital would have ground to a standstill many years ago).

But that's not to say the Tube is averse to a spot of moonlighting and, when it's not been conveying commuters to their destination, the Underground has played a major role in freight transportation across – or more accurately beneath – the capital.

There are far fewer freight trains in service today than back in their post-war heyday but every now and then unsuspecting travellers can still be waiting on the platform for the next train to West Ruislip to emerge from the tunnel only to see a scruffy freight locomotive appear, dragging its cargo of gravel or assorted building materials.

The height of the Tube's freight foray was in the 1950s. The Metropolitan Line ran three trains a day on the Uxbridge branch to transport coal while the Circle Line was once no stranger to British Railways engines carrying goods on its tracks.

Most freight trains on the Underground ran at night to avoid clashing with their commuter cousins and causing congestion on the network. This included the engines that ran along the Metropolitan Line, which used to deliver cattle to Smithfield Meat Market right up until the 1960s.

Freight could yet enjoy a renaissance on the Underground. With London's roads slower and more congested than ever, the 'London Freight Plan' is already investigating alternative ways of getting goods to where they need to be. At night-time particularly, the Tube could well be the answer.

FA CUP TAKES
THE TUBE
1964

You've probably got more chance of spotting alien life on the Underground than catching a glimpse of a modern Premier League footballer who, naturally, wouldn't be seen dead on public transport and absolutely must travel everywhere in a car that costs at least £100,000.

It was different in the old days, though, and if you happened to be on the Tube on 2 May 1964, you might just have witnessed a bizarre sight as West Ham United manager Ron Greenwood headed home after the FA Cup final.

In front of a crowd of 100,000, Greenwood's Hammers side had just beaten Preston North End 3-2 at Wembley with a dramatic 90th-minute winner from Ronnie Boyce, and there was no shortage of champagne in the dressing room after the game as the celebrations began.

But Greenwood wasn't the party animal and as his players prepared to find the nearest nightclub, he picked up the FA Cup and jumped on the Tube. Cunningly, he wrapped the trophy in a cloth to avoid getting mobbed and both he and the famous silverware made it back to *chez* Greenwood unscathed.

There were even more celebrations later in the year when a West End cinema decided to show highlights of the victory and Greenwood and the trophy were the guests of honour. But rather than book a limo for the event, the Hammers' boss took the Tube with the legendary silverware cunningly wrapped in a cloth to avoid undue attention.

There is, for those who may doubt the story, a famous black-and-white picture of Greenwood sitting on a bench at Tottenham

Court Road Station, with the incognito FA Cup nestled safely on his lap.

The beautiful game and the network did come together again in 2005 with the release of the film *Green Street* but it was a less-than-beautiful reunion with the movie depicting graphic football hooliganism.

The Underground scenes were filmed at East Finchley Station on the Northern Line and against the critical odds the movie won a number of awards, including the Best of the Fest at the Malibu Film Festival and the Special Jury Award at the South by Southwest Film Festival.

Football and (play) acting have continued to enjoy a close relationship ever since and most modern players have now perfected their 'shot by a sniper' routine and happily entertain the fans with it every time they stray into the opposition penalty area.

VICTORY FOR THE
VICTORIA LINE
1968

The problem with building new Tube lines is that as soon as the tunnelling is finished, the new ticket barriers have been installed and you've trained up an army of *Evening Standard* distributors, the whole thing gets clogged up with pesky passengers and the problem of congestion rears its ugly head again.

Such was the dilemma in London after the Second World War as the Underground struggled to cope with the number of commuters spilling in and out of the carriages, so in 1948 the British Transport Commission set up a working party to investigate the feasibility of running a track from Victoria to Walthamstow. They didn't know it, but the Victoria Line was now in the pipeline.

The idea was not met with universal approval and the debate on how to alleviate the capital's growing public transport crisis dragged on for years, culminating in a radical alternative proposal from Harold Watkinson, the MP for Woking and a government minister.

'It [the Victoria Line] would cost £55 million,' he argued in 1959. 'The question to be decided, and upon which I wish to take the advice of the London Travel Committee, is whether this £55 million would pay a better dividend were it spent on off-street parking.'

The car park idea had supporters in Westminster, but Conservative Prime Minister Harold Macmillan was worried about unemployment and reasoned a new Tube line would create more jobs, particularly for the Northeast shipyards who would land the steelwork contracts, than simply concreting more of London to accommodate cars.

Macmillan's intervention was decisive and in 1962 work began, the Victoria Line opening six years later. The National Car Parks company weren't happy but the newly connected residents of Vauxhall and Pimlico, Seven Sisters and Tottenham Hale were over the moon.

History has certainly vindicated Macmillan's decision to ignore the vocal car lobby. Today an estimated 200 million passengers use the Victoria line each and every year, which would require an awful lot of multi-storey car parks – not to mention the driving gloves, mints and fluffy dice – were the commuters forced to make those journeys by road rather than rail.

These days the Victoria Line even has its own Twitter account, reflecting its status as one of the network's newest and most 'with it' lines, although the Tweets do tend to focus on service updates and passenger information rather than abusing celebrities or the sale of dubious medical remedies for the older gentleman.

PLEASE MIND THE GAP
1968

The London Underground is an engineering and architectural masterpiece that still stands as testimony to the skill, ingenuity and vision of those who conceived, designed and ultimately built the world's biggest subterranean transport system.

It's got its faults, though. The stifling heat in the summer, the constant noise levels and lack of space are all definite negatives and then there is the curious case of the dreaded gap, the ominous and life-threatening void between the carriage and the platform at certain stations on the network.

The gaps are the result of various engineering oddities. Some arise when 'straight' rolling stock arrives at a station with a curved platform, while other spaces are created because of platforms which have to accommodate both deep-level and sub-level trains, which are marginally different heights. The gap at Bank Station is reported to be so big because the tunnel diggers had to ensure they didn't encroach on the nearby Bank of England vaults.

Until 1968, diligent drivers would remind passengers they were one misguided step away from oblivion each time they left the train, but that all seemed a bit archaic and London Underground finally decided to record a safety message. Hence the legendary 'Mind the Gap' reprise was invented.

The first voice commuters heard imploring them not to plummet beneath the train belonged to sound engineer Peter Lodge. He had originally been asked to help record an actor speaking the words, but the acquisitive thesp suddenly demanded royalties every time his message was played and London Underground understandably told him to take a running jump. Lodge had already recorded the phrase to test sound levels on the equipment and Tube bosses decided that it was cheaper to stick with his effort rather than bother Equity again.

Lodge's dulcet tones were soon heard across the network helping to save life and limb, but he's not the only person to record the message. Tim Bentinck, a.k.a. David Archer in Radio 4's *The Archers*, is the man behind the voice on Piccadilly Line trains, while the phrase got the feminine touch in 1999 when Emma Clarke hit the recording studio.

The working relationship lasted eight years but all ended rather acrimoniously in 2007 when an interview in the *Daily Mail* seemed to suggest Clarke was not exactly an avid fan of Underground commuting and everyone got rather hot under the collar. Clarke claimed she'd been misquoted, Transport for London claimed she'd betrayed them and her P45 was in the post before she could say 'the next station is West Brompton'.

'Mind the Gap', however, has done quite well without her and is now used on transport systems from Brazil to China, Sweden and Portugal, proving gaps really are an international menace.

The phrase has also permeated into popular culture with at least four books, a movie production company, a theatre company and a board game having 'borrowed' the three little words of warning for their own name.

Minding the gap, it seems, has never been so popular.

THE MISPLACED PISTOLS
OF FINSBURY PARK

1968

Passengers who regularly use Finsbury Park Station on the Victoria Line will be familiar with the elegant tile motif on the platform that depicts a pair of duelling pistols, but most commuters probably don't realise the guns really shouldn't be there.

The pistols were commissioned by London Underground for the new Finsbury Park Station, which was opened in 1968 when the Victoria Line came into service. English poster artist Tom Eckersley was approached to design an eye-catching motif and, in a nod to the area's history as a site for duelling in the early nineteenth century, it was decided a pistols theme would be appropriate.

Which would make a nice story were it not for the fact London Underground dropped a bit of an historical clanger and confused Finsbury *Park* for Finsbury *Fields*, a more central location in Islington that really was used by disgruntled toffs with shooters to settle their arguments.

All 16 of the new Victoria Line stations were adorned with tile mosaics back in the 1960s but thankfully there were no more embarrassing mistakes, which explains why the network boasts a silhouette of Queen Victoria at Victoria and a black horse motif at, well, Blackhorse Road Station.

Brixton has a pile of bricks – an artistic play on words – while Oxford Circus is decorated with a geometric snakes and ladders motif of blue, red and brown dots to represent how people change between the Victoria, Central and Bakerloo Lines through a maze of passageways.

Thankfully, a motif for Cockfosters was never commissioned.

THE DARK SIDE OF TUBE TRAVEL
1972

Although the barrage of CCTV cameras ensure the London Underground is statistically one of the safest forms of public transport, there is still something a little eerie and sinister about the Tube should you find yourself all alone on a deserted platform, cut off from the world above.

The sense of menace has led to many macabre urban myths about the network, but perhaps the most well-worn is the terrifying tale of the young woman who gets on a train late at night and only narrowly escapes meeting with a grisly fate.

The women, the story goes, gets onto the carriage to find just one other passenger, a young man, on board. At the next stop, however, two men carry what seems like a sleeping woman onto the train and as it rumbles on, the first man approaches the lady passenger and whispers conspiratorially in her ear, 'Get off at the next stop.'

She's obviously suspicious but, glancing at the other three late-night commuters, she senses something is seriously wrong and decides to take his advice. The pair disembark and as she looks nervously at the departing carriage, she sees the back of the trio's heads and suddenly notices a pair of scissors sticking out of the dead women's skull.

The Underground has also been both the inspiration and setting for two rather gruesome horror films and those of a nervous disposition who are also regular Tube users would be well advised to stop reading now.

The first – *Death Line* – was released in 1972 and tells the unsettling story of a family of cannibals descended from Victorian railway workers who live in the network's dark tunnels and feast on unsuspecting passengers at Russell Square and Holborn. The flesh-eaters, however, make a big mistake when they kidnap and devour an important politician and are subsequently hunted down by the Met's finest.

In 2004, *Creep* was premiered and had the stomachs of audiences churning with its graphic portrayal of a young woman who accidentally gets locked in overnight at an Underground station and is subsequently mercilessly stalked by a hideously deformed and deranged serial killer (a.k.a. Creep), who butchers anyone she meets almost as soon as she can cry, 'Can you help me?'

Needless to say, she eventually escapes his murderous clutches, there are no other survivors (although a cute dog does make it out) and the villain meets a suitably over-the-top and anatomically revealing end.

In literature, the dark side of the Tube was celebrated in 2010 with the publication of an anthology of terrifying tales entitled *The End of the Line*.

'This collection of stories from some of horror fiction's best authors will glue you to the page,' promised the press release. 'But watch out, it may leave you too afraid to take the metro to work. In deep tunnels something stirs, borne on a warm breath of wind, reeking of diesel and blood. The spaces between stations hold secrets too terrible for the upper world to comprehend and the steel lines sing with the songs of the dead.'

It's probably safe to assume they're not talking about Elvis's greatest hits.

COMMUTERS GET A CULINARY SURPRISE
1979

The London Underground is not, by any stretch of the imagination, renowned for its excellent cuisine. If you're lucky you might find yourself tucking into a bag of cheese and onion crisps from a vending machine, but if you're really unfortunate you'll be forced to sit next to an inebriated idiot chomping their way through a particularly smelly takeaway on the journey home.

In short, the Tube and good food are virtual strangers.

But that all briefly changed in May 1979 when the Jubilee Line was opened to the public for the first time and the unsuspecting passengers who boarded one of the new trains at Bond Street Station were offered a delicious cordon bleu meal. On a real plate.

The commuters wolfed down their meal accompanied by the strains of a string quartet, who had been parachuted in to add a touch of elegance to proceedings, and everyone agreed that the Jubilee Line was without doubt a class above the network's other lines.

Sadly, they got the shock of their lives the following day when they arrived at Bond Street to discover it was back to business as usual and the only free food on offer was a half-eaten ham sandwich thrown on the carriage floor.

At least the lucky passengers who did get a gratis lunch had a better experience of the grand opening than poor old Prince Charles, who was bundled into a driver's cab in one of the new trains for an awkward photo opportunity.

The pictures of the heir apparent smiling inanely in the cab are truly terrible and made a nonsense of the argument that Charles wasn't earning his annual Civil List salary.

A QUICK PINT ON
THE PLATFORM
1985

A long, hot Tube journey can force even the most hardened Underground commuter to turn to drink and until 1985, dehydrated passengers didn't even have to leave Sloane Square Station to quench their thirst.

Like many other stations on the network, Sloane Square boasted its very own pub. Called the 'Hole In The Wall', the watering hole was on the westbound platform of the station and was so famous it features heavily in the 1975 book *A Word Child* by Iris Murdoch.

'After leaving the office I would travel either to Sloane Square or to Liverpool Street to have a drink in the station buffet,' the lead character relates.

> In the whole extension of the Underground system those two stations are, as far as I've been able to discover, the only ones which have bars actually upon the platform. The concept of the tube station platform bar excited me.
>
> In fact the whole Underground region moved me, I felt as if it were in some sense my natural home. These two bars were not just a cosy after-the-office treat, they were the source of a dark excitement, places of profound communication with London, with the sources of life, with the caverns of resignation to grief and to mortality.
>
> Drinking there between six and seven in the shifting crowds of rush-hour travellers, one could feel on one's shoulder as a curiously soothing yoke the weariness of toiling London, that blanked released tiredness after work which can somehow console even the bored, even the frenzied.

There were at one time more than 30 licensed premises on the Tube, which were often open outside normal licensing hours, but sadly one by one they were closed down as London Underground decided that hordes of tipsy travellers wandering around the network was an accident waiting to happen.

London Mayor Boris Johnson went a step further in 2008 when he banned alcohol on the network completely, ensuring sobriety rather than silliness was the order of the day.

ANIMAL MAP MAGIC
1988

Join-the-dots has been a simple childhood favourite for decades but it also happens to be the inspiration for an unusual art project and merchandising operation based on Harry Beck's iconic Tube map.

'Animals On The Underground' began life in 1988 when illustrator Paul Middlewick was using the network and suddenly realised he could create the outlines of a series of creatures simply by joining up the map's lines, stations and junctions.

'I got the idea when I was travelling on the Tube,' Middlewick said. 'It gets very boring commuting daily on the Underground and I'd stare at the map as I waited for my train. After a while, I started to see shapes in the Tube map, particularly animals. I sketched them down and "Animals On The Underground" was born.

'Since then, I have picked out over 20 different animals from the intersecting lines and stations on the map. My favourite animal has to be the Elephant. He's the first animal I spotted and remains, to me at least, the cutest one.

'I do have loads of other animals, possibly as many as 50. However, I set myself very high standards and only publish the ones I feel are good enough for everyone to enjoy. I still surprise myself by spotting new ones. I have spotted other items such as bottles, buildings and vehicles but it's always the animals which are the most memorable and appealing.'

His creations range from the everyday to the exotic and all are prefixed by the name of one of the stations found within the design, meaning visitors to his website can feast their eyes on the Queen's Park Cat and Barking the Dog, as well as the Whitechapel Polar Bear and Hornchurch the Rhino.

Since coming up with the idea, Middlewick has marketed a series of T-shirts showcasing his creations and 'Animals On The

Underground' has made quite an impression on popular culture. In 2003, the concept was used in a poster campaign to advertise London Zoo and in 2008 the International Fund for Animal Welfare ran a poster campaign using Middlewick's seal, elephant and whale images to raise awareness of illegal hunting. In 2010 a children's book called Lost Property was published featuring characters called Elephant & Castle and Angel the Angel Fish.

So next time you're staring blankly at a Tube map, why not see how many you can find?

FARE-DODGING PIGEONS
1995

Pigeons are extremely intelligent creatures. They know, for example, exactly when you've just had your car cleaned or you're about to enjoy a sandwich on a park bench, while their ability to find their way home from over hundreds of miles away is legendary.

And now it seems our feathered friends have added another trick to their impressive repertoire – travelling on the Underground.

Reports of pigeons casually hopping on and off the Tube first surfaced in 1995, and ever since sightings of the birds commuting up and down the network (without ever buying a ticket) have been flooding in.

'Pigeons are catching the Underground to save flying time across London, according to a flurry of correspondence to a scientific journal,' reported the *Daily Telegraph*, continuing:

> The letters were triggered when Rachel Robson of Bayswater wrote to describe how she saw a pigeon board a Tube train and travel one stop from Paddington. 'With their renowned navigational abilities, is it possible the pigeon knew where it was going?' she wrote to the *New Scientist*.
>
> The birds are not blundering into the trains, but deliberately hopping on board to save time and energy commuting across London, according to letters published yesterday. Unfortunately for the birds, travel does have its drawbacks. 'Pigeons are classified as vermin,' said a spokesman for London Underground. 'If they are caught they should be destroyed.'

The Tube's pigeon passengers were caught on camera in 2012 by the BBC programme *Natural World: Unnatural History of London*, but opinion remains split whether the birds are travelling in search of food or have simply become too lazy to fly around the capital.

Pigeons have become such a problem on the Underground that TfL has been forced to employ drastic measures to scare them off. At Paddington Station, Sally the hawk is unleashed three times a week to intimidate her feathered cousins while the roof of Wembley Park Station is adorned with a series of fake owls to 'persuade' the local pigeons to take up residence elsewhere.

In 1999 the bosses at TfL were so worried that the opening of the Millennium Dome and North Greenwich Tube Station would be ruined by unwelcome pigeon deposits that they drafted in Hamish the Harris hawk to ensure everything would remain nice and clean.

'He doesn't kill the birds,' insisted Wayne Davis, Hamish's owner. 'He's a deterrent, so we do the job without guns or poison. Pigeons don't only foul and damage buildings – they spread tuberculosis, salmonella, ornithosis and other respiratory diseases to humans.'

Perhaps something to think of before you next throw one a bit of your sandwich ...

BEWARE THE TUBE'S NEW BREED OF BITING BUG

1998

The miles of dark and invitingly damp tunnels of the London Underground produced a startling revelation in 1998 when scientists discovered the network was home to a previously undiscovered species of rather moody mosquito.

The new breed was quickly christened *Culex pipiens f. molestus* in recognition of its voracious appetite for biting the Tube's resident mice and rats – not to mention beleaguered maintenance workers – and scientists were particularly stunned when they realised these subterranean insects were a separate species from their above-ground relatives.

Mosquitoes first found their way beneath the surface of the capital when the Underground's tunnels were dug over a century ago, attracted by the system's warm conditions and pools of stagnant water for breeding, but scientists assumed the subterranean adventurers had simply adapted to life in the depths rather than evolved into a new species.

That all changed in 1998 when tests conducted by Kate Byrne and Richard Nichols of Queen Mary & Westfield College in London confirmed that the Tube dwellers had developed into something altogether different.

'It's a remarkable story of evolution,' said Roz Cox, editor of the BBC's *Wildlife* magazine. 'The scientists say that the differences between the above- and below-ground forms are as great as if the species had been separated for thousands of years.'

Attempts to mate the two species failed, despite suitably low lighting and romantic music, and the only conclusion was that the Underground's unique ecosystem had speeded up the natural evolution process, creating a new breed in the space of 150 years that can now only survive down in the Underground's tunnels.

The original, above-ground mosquitoes feed on birds rather than mammals but their underground counterparts quickly switched their diet to the plentiful supply of rodents, as well as any unfortunate Tube staff tasked with working below the streets of London.

The first bites from *Culex pipiens f. molestus* were recorded during the Second World War when people took refuge from the Blitz on the system's deserted platforms.

But while the London Tube appears to have been the first to experience the unwelcome attentions of the bug, it is not the world's only underground system to be affected by the upstart insect and in the summer of 2011, the New York subway was also plagued by the newly discovered scientific oddity. Being on the other side of the Atlantic, however, the American subway mosquitoes were naturally bigger than their Tube cousins.

THE WATER HOLES THAT SAVE LIVES
1999

Suicides on the London Underground are, tragically, a regular occurrence but the mortality rate beneath the streets of the capital would be much, much higher were it not for a strange quirk of fate concerning the Tube's original design and the need to stop the network flooding.

Most platforms at the deepest stations on the Tube were designed with pits beneath the track to help drain away unexpected water but they now serve as unintentional but hugely welcome life-savers when passengers jump – or indeed fall – in front of a speeding train.

Now officially known as 'anti-suicide pits', but colloquially called 'dead man's trenches', the metre-deep drainage pits allow trains to drive over the stricken passenger without always causing fatality or serious injury. According to a study by doctors at the Royal London Hospital in 1999, the mortality rate on the tracks at stations with the old pits was half that of those without them.

'Being hit by a train is an important cause of death from trauma in London,' explained Tim Coats, a senior lecturer in accident and emergency medicine at the hospital (deploying what some might view as a novel use of the word 'important'). 'The mechanics of the interaction of the human body with the train are poorly studied and so present rolling stock and stations are not designed to maximise survival.'

It is impossible to calculate exactly how many lives have been saved by the pits since the Tube was opened in the nineteenth century but were it not for their existence, many more people would surely have met with a grisly end on the Underground.

CLEANERS WITH A HEAD FOR HEIGHTS

1999

Westminster Station on the Circle and District Line is one of the busiest on the network and its platforms are frequently crammed with tourists desperate for that all-important holiday snap of the Houses of Parliament or politicians eager to demonstrate a vote-winning common touch.

The sub-surface platforms were opened in 1868 by the Metropolitan District Railway but it wasn't until 1999 that the deep-level section of the station was unveiled as part of the Jubilee Line extension, a masterpiece of modern architecture featuring wall-to-wall stainless-steel tubes and concrete supports.

It's what you'd call seriously eye-catching and the awards duly poured in, winning the Royal Fine Art Commission Millennium Building of the Year gong in 2000, the Civic Trust award for design in 2000 and 2002 and the RIBA Award for Architecture in 2001.

Praise indeed, but what the architects didn't take into account as they were hunched over their drawing boards was exactly how Transport for London would go about actually cleaning the bloody thing!

The problem is, those steel arches are so high there's not a feather duster in the world long enough to reach all the lofty nooks and crevices. TfL has been forced to take drastic measures to tackle the dust – employing a four-man team of abseilers to come in and clean the station.

'To reach many parts of the station like the sides of the escalators, pipes and high-up empty spaces, specially qualified cleaners must abseil when the station is closed to passengers,' explained TfL.

The climbers are deployed annually for an 8-to-10-week stint to get the job done and are also responsible for changing all the light bulbs to ensure the tourists and politicians are not left fumbling in the dark.

THE PRIME MINISTER'S TRAVEL CONUNDRUM

1999

When the first section of the Metropolitan Line was opened to the public in 1863, there was quite a commotion. The construction of the four-mile line between Farringdon and Paddington had already piqued people's interest in the new subterranean form of transport and by nine o'clock on the morning of 10 January, the Metropolitan Line was bursting at the seams with curious commuters.

The *Spectator* magazine reported that Londoners would rather ride the new trains than the 'horrible sarcophagi known as omnibuses' while *The Times* took a dimmer view, dismissing the Tube as 'an insult to common sense to suppose that people would ever prefer to be driven amid palpable darkness through the foul subsoil of London.'

Opinion may have been divided but the sheer numbers spoke for themselves and 30,000 took a ride on the Underground that first day. The prime minister of the day, Lord Palmerston, was not among them however, having turned down an invitation to make the inaugural journey.

The 78-year-old Liberal politician was definitely not an Underground fan and refused to attend the grand opening, arguing he intended to spend whatever time he had left in his life above rather than beneath ground.

It was advice Tony Blair probably wished he had followed when he unwisely decided to take the Tube in 1999, a PR gambit that backfired so spectacularly that for once even the Prime Minister's famous smile failed him.

Tony was travelling on the Jubilee Line extension to see how the Millennium Dome was coming along, accompanied of course by a horde of reporters and photographers, when he spotted a commuter minding her own business and tried to start up an impromptu conversation to prove what a thoroughly down-to-earth chap he was.

The poor passenger – Georgina Leketi-Solomon – was appalled at the flagrant breach of Tube etiquette and ignored all of Tony's saccharin advances, staring straight ahead listening to her Walkman (which, for the younger reader, was a two-ton portable music playing device used in the dark days before iPods).

The Prime Minister went redder than his party conference tie as the photographers caught his obvious discomfort while Georgina bolted for the door at the next station.

'I did realise it was him but it all seemed a bit overwhelming at quarter past nine in the morning,' she said later. 'It's not exactly what you expect on the way to work. I'm always the same in the mornings, I put my Walkman on and turn off. All my friends have been teasing me, telling me I shouldn't talk to strange men.'

Or vote for them.

MADELEINE GETS UP COMMUTERS' NOSES

2001

Let's face it, the Underground isn't always the most pleasant experience when it comes to aromas. There's always at least one passenger with dubious personal hygiene for every carriage and as people cram into every available space during the hot summer months, the Tube frequently makes a mockery of those adverts for deodorants promising 24-hour protection.

It was a problem giving the management bods at London Underground particularly sleepless nights back in 2001 until one ingenious soul hit upon the idea of unleashing a perfumed dubbed 'Madeleine' on unsuspecting commuters in the hope of masking the worst whiffs.

Everyone thought it was a great idea and in April the platforms at St James's Park, Euston and Piccadilly were coated with a special residue designed to release what they hoped was a pleasant smell as passengers walked on them.

'We carry more than three million passengers a day and the atmosphere down in our stations can become an interesting collection of odours reflecting all aspects of London life,' said customer services director Mike Brown. 'Some are nice, some not so nice. That's why we are trialling Madeleine to see if a refresher will make a positive difference. If it's a hit, it could become a permanent item.'

The intrepid reporters of the BBC were duly despatched down the Tube on the first day of the trial to canvas opinion and the reaction, in truth, was mixed. 'I think the smell is good,' admitted one commuter. 'I think it will have a universal appeal to both men and women as it is not too florally.' Another passenger was not so enthusiastic. 'It smells like flowers or pollen,' he said. 'But I think the best idea to get rid of the smells is to deodorise the people instead.'

An initial score draw perhaps, but defeat was just around the corner as complaints began to flood in that the smell was making people feel sick. Rather than risk what could turn into a messy bout of subterranean nausea, the idea was quietly shelved.

A clear case of London Underground spectacularly failing to come up smelling of roses.

MUSIC TO SOOTHE THE SAVAGE COMMUTER
2001

Music may indeed soothe the savage beast (or, more accurately, breast) but commuters on the Tube can be an irritable bunch at the best of times and sometimes not even the melodic strains of Ralph McTell's 'Streets of London' or 'Going Underground' by The Jam drifting across the platform are enough to becalm a throng of disgruntled passengers.

Not that the network's buskers don't do their level best to cheer them up, and ever since 2001 the city's street musicians have been feverishly strumming their guitars with the full approval of the suits at Transport for London.

Before then busking on the Tube was illegal and anyone found performing on the system was quickly moved on, fined and potentially imprisoned in a never-ending game of cat-and-mouse between the musicians and Underground staff. In 2001, however, TfL decided to call a truce and award licences to approved buskers.

The initiative needed a celebrity for the big launch. Sadly Elton John and David Bowie were busy so classical musician Julian Lloyd Webber, Andrew's younger brother, was asked to bring his cello along to Westminster Station and perform a few numbers.

'I am delighted to be able to launch the Underground system as a brand-new platform for the performing arts in this country,' Julian said as someone dropped 10p in his cello case. 'I hope that this will inspire all sorts of musicians from all walks of life to bring their music, whether it be classical, musicals, pop, folk, reggae, jazz and the like, to a wider audience.

'I have been in London all my life so the Tube is part of my everyday life. What I do not like is those guys who come with a pre-recorded tape to play to. I think it is good that there should be some quality control. The last thing that you want if you have got a headache or a hangover is someone who cannot play.'

Around 250 buskers now perform on the Underground every day on instruments as diverse as violins, steel drums, harmonicas and accordions. Which all still sound absolutely awful if you do happen to be nursing a particularly nasty hangover.

The burning question for most buskers, however, has to be which song is the most profitable? After all, parting passengers from their money is the name of the game and in 2005 music bible *Q* conducted a survey to try and find the elusive answer.

The magazine despatched a busker by the name of Diamond Dave below the streets of the capital with a playlist; after a few hours' strumming away, he returned to the surface with the results of the Underground jury.

It transpired the least lucrative song was 'Motorcycle Emptiness' by the Manic Street Preachers, yielding a measly 32p. Surprisingly, Queen's classic 'Bohemian Rhapsody' fared little better with an 86p return, while the Kinks' apt 'Waterloo Sunset' earned Dave £1.50 and an out-of-date travelcard.

At the other end of the scale, 'Strawberry Fields Forever' by some band called the Beatles was rewarded with £2.46 in commuter contributions while a rendition of Elvis Costello's 'Oliver's Army' was apparently worth a healthy £3.82.

But the clear winner in terms of cash was 'Wonderwall' by Oasis, which persuaded passengers to cough up a grand total of £7.45, proof positive that hailing from Manchester is no barrier to success in the capital.

THE BABY THAT WAS REALLY A MONKEY

2001

The Underground has inspired countless novelists but one of the strangest tomes written about the network is Christopher Ross's *Tunnel Visions*, published in 2001, a fascinating and funny first-hand account of his surreal experiences working as a Tube station assistant at Oxford Circus.

A former lawyer, oriental carpet smuggler, camel cowboy and Japanese soap actor, Ross took the job expecting a sedate, uneventful life beneath the streets of the capital but quickly discovered there was rarely a dull moment when working on the Underground.

His most bizarre stories include the idiotic passenger at Green Park who was told it would be quicker to walk to Oxford Circus than to wait for the next train and promptly set off down the tunnel, somehow avoiding electrocuting himself on the live rail, and the incredibly ugly baby on a carriage that turned out to be a monkey.

A commuter travelling with a domesticated fox on a dog's lead and the sad story of the suicide who took the advice of his Nike shirt and just did it also feature to make a compelling, if at times disturbing read.

'*Tunnel Visions* is a delightful mixture of lived experience in the surreal world of London's Underground and the more elevated ideas, thoughts and imaginings that experience provokes,' reads the book's Amazon review. 'Oxford Circus Station, complete with its weeping wall, its streakers, buskers, onanists and cupboard containing one employee whose ideal working day was to sleep soundly 100 feet below ground, is a Plato's Cave of reflection and human comedy. Christopher Ross, a still point in the whirling stream of the bizarre and otherworldly life below ground, has written a profoundly funny book.'

Ross spent 16 months in the employ of Transport for London and, when it comes to the Tube, *Tunnel Visions* proves that fact really is stranger than fiction.

VASECTOMY BRINGS CIRCLE LINE TO A STANDSTILL

2003

The number of different reasons for delays to trains on the Underground are almost as plentiful as passengers who use the network, but few have been quite as bizarre as the cause of the disruption to the service in 2003 just outside Aldgate Station.

The train in question was being driven by a trainee under the watchful eye of an instructor and a senior driver but when the two older men began discussing (in graphic detail) a recent vasectomy one of them had undergone, things started to go very wrong.

The squeamish young trainee begged his colleagues to change the subject of conversation but they ignored his desperate request and, moments later, he was overwhelmed by their unsettling medical conversation and fainted.

Unfortunately, when he lost consciousness he fell out of the window of the moving cab, hit the tracks and sustained head and chest injuries that hospitalised him.

Mercifully the train was only travelling at 15mph at the time and the trainee made a full recovery, but both the Hammersmith & City and Circle Lines were brought to a complete standstill as his ashen-faced colleagues slammed on the brakes and waited for the paramedics to arrive.

Transport for London initially blamed the delays on a defective train but details of how a vasectomy had actually ruined the journey of thousands of unsuspecting commuters soon emerged. The sniggers could be heard up and down the network for days but it did at least make a refreshing change from a points failure or leaves on the line.

POST OFFICE GOES UNDERGROUND

2003

The Underground may be synonymous with sub-surface transport in the capital but it is in fact not the only subterranean system down there. For 75 years, the Post Office operated its own railway underneath the city to ensure Londoners received their utility bills and junk mail every morning

Dubbed 'Mail Rail', the network ran for six and a half miles from Whitechapel to Paddington, serving the main sorting offices along the route, and for nearly eight decades the train took the strain, conveying millions of letters and parcels beneath London and avoiding clogging the roads with Post Office vans.

The idea first began to germinate in 1908 when a team of Post Office engineers paid a visit to the Chicago Freight subway system and all agreed subterranean transport was a jolly good plan. The team continued their research with a trip to Germany to analyse another sub-surface network and they returned to Blighty convinced Mail Rail was the future.

As the Post Office didn't have a track record in digging tunnels they approached the Underground Electric Railways Company of London for advice and expertise, and the Tube bigwigs agreed to help with the ambitious work.

The network finally opened in December 1927 just in time for the Christmas rush and at its peak it was running 19 hours a day, 286 days a year, carrying an astonishing 4 million letters daily on fully automated, driverless trains on a mere 2ft-gauge track.

Mail Rail had a good innings but by the early twenty-first century it was beginning to struggle to make ends meet. When Royal Mail revealed the system had become five times more expensive than using London's roads, the writing was on the wall, and in May 2003 the network was reluctantly mothballed.

'My last shift is on Friday and then my colleagues on nights will close it down on Saturday morning,' Mail Rail's Amanda Smith said in the final week before closure. 'I doubt we'll give the railway a send-off this week as we'll be too upset to do anything.

'I'm based at the Mount Pleasant sorting office in Farringdon, where the station is about 70 feet below ground. Coming out of the lift onto the platform, it looks not dissimilar to the London Underground. The station is a miniature version of the Tube at platform level although the trains themselves are nothing like Tube trains. There's no driver, for one thing.

'We used to have big Christmas parties down here for kids from the local children's home with the platform decorated like Santa's Grotto and this secret train for delivering presents.

'There's a passenger carriage that only comes out for special occasions and I cadged a lift on it one day. We rode from here to Paddington and it was quite a bumpy ride. We were all packed in tight – we had to sit two to a row – but at least that stopped us rolling about too much. In between stations it was often pitch-black, so it was like London's biggest ghost ride.'

In theory Mail Rail could be resurrected at any time but the explosion in new-fangled hi-tech forms of communication make a Lazarus-like reanimation unlikely.

Members of the public are not allowed to venture down the tunnels and see the remnants of Mail Rail for themselves but for those whose interest has been piqued, the network does make a cameo in Bruce Willis's 1991 action comedy *Hudson Hawk*, masquerading as a private railway beneath the Vatican City.

The film failed to deliver at the box office, an accusation that certainly could not be levelled at the Post Office's ground-breaking service.

THE TUBE'S PHANTOM POLICEMAN

2003

The long arm of the law is often a reassuring sight but seasoned Underground travellers will grimly warn that you never want to come across an 'Inspector Sands' while journeying on the Tube.

And that's because 'Inspector Sands' isn't a member of the Met or the British Transport Police but a coded Tannoy message used by Underground staff when there is a fire alert or suspicious package on the network.

The secretive nature of the announcement is intended to avoid alarming commuters, but there is a suspicion that regular Tube travellers have rumbled Transport for London's less-than-subtle ruse.

'Today there can hardly be a single regular traveller on public transport in London who doesn't realise that when the man on the Tannoy demands the urgent presence of Inspector Sands, what he means is that the nearest officer from Special Branch or the Bomb Squad should go immediately to the place specified,' Tom Utley wrote in the *Daily Telegraph* in 2003. 'We seasoned commuters look at each other and smile. And when we smile, we are telling each other this: "Aw, bless them! They are trying not to frighten us. But we know exactly what they mean. And still we are not scared."'

The exact wording of the announcement varies from station to station but it is always preferable to hear that 'Inspector Sands' has in fact left the building rather than that he's heading in your direction with three fire engines in tow.

PERILS OF THE OYSTER CARD
2003

Former London Mayor Ken Livingstone looked like the cat who'd got the cream in 2003 when he proudly launched the Oyster card, promising a new era of hassle-free travel around the city and no doubt hoping that his shiny new electronic swipe card would help earn him a second term as the capital's head honcho.

He was half-right. London's commuters were sufficiently impressed with Ken's fancy new 'ticketless' ticket to vote him back as mayor in 2004, but the new-fangled Oyster cards were not exactly without hassle as it gradually became apparent that the electronic fingerprint from the cards could be put to unintended uses.

What people began to realise was that anyone could key in a card's serial number on a website to reveal the details of every journey made using that card on London's public transport in the last 10 weeks, and suddenly suspicious spouses from Barnet to Balham were going online to check exactly where their loved ones had been.

'Oyster cards won't tell you that the bloke's been cheating on his wife but it will show if he's been in one part of town when he's supposed to be somewhere else,' said one private investigator interviewed by the *Independent* in 2006. 'It is an easy thing to confront your partner with. It doesn't look like you've been snooping around too much.'

Things got more serious when the boys in blue began examining people's Oyster card records as part of criminal investigations, and the familiar Big Brother debate was reignited before you could say CCTV.

In 2004 the Met made a modest seven requests to TfL for journey information but in January 2006 the police came calling 61 times for the Oyster information stored on the Underground's computers, sparking a rabid response from our brave freedom fighters.

'I think it's outrageous,' raged Heather Brooke from Privacy International. 'Londoners are already the most watched people on earth. If the police can't conduct effective investigations with a CCTV camera on every corner, then that's really indicative of a more serious problem with police investigations.'

TfL blushed awkwardly and then issued a response that the police absolutely, definitely had not written for them. 'Big Brother is not watching you,' it read. 'We collect journey data so we can provide customer service and answer customer queries. A by-product of that is that the data is on record if the police seek records in individual cases but we only provide that data in response to a written request from the police that is then reviewed on a case-by-case basis.'

Still, anyone of a paranoid disposition travelling on the Tube might be advised to pay cash.

WHO'D TRAVEL IN A LIFT LIKE THIS?

2004

A TV presenter turned purveyor of tasty but eye-wateringly expensive cooking sauces, Loyd Grossman made his name in the 1980s by invading the homes and privacy of desperate celebrities in ITV's *Through the Keyhole*, annoying a nation with his mid-Atlantic drawl, smugness and maddening catchphrase.

Little did the hapless commuters and innocent tourists who found themselves using Covent Garden Station in 2004 realise, however, that even on the London Underground there was to be absolutely no escape from Grossman's voice.

Covent Garden is the busiest station on the network that is only accessible by lifts (apart from emergency stairs) and when Tube bosses agreed to pipe in a recorded message from Grossman urging the trapped and helpless to visit a nearby museum, they really were shooting fish in a barrel.

'Turn right into the Piazza,' Grossman urged before the irate travellers lost the will to live, 'for one of my favourite museums – the London Transport Museum.'

Exactly how many people followed the recorded advice is unrecorded but sales of earplugs around Covent Garden spiked shortly after the message was rolled out.

'Covent Garden is one of London's most exciting destinations,' Loyd explained in lieu of a proper defence for his actions. 'It's a feast of culture, shopping, food and performance and one of my favourite museums, London's Transport Museum, is at its heart.'

Which was all technically true but totally irrelevant as yet another passenger was hauled from the lifts and strapped into a straitjacket for their own safety.

THE HOLBORN FAUX PAS
2005

Holborn Station has many claims to fame. It is the only station on the network that serves both the Central and Piccadilly Lines, its frontage is made from Portland stone rather than the standard red terracotta common in the area and it was responsible for the demise of the famed British Museum Station, which closed in 1933 when nearby Holborn was expanded.

It featured in the video for Suede's 1997 hit 'Saturday Night' and also appeared in a scene in Mike Leigh's critically acclaimed film *Secrets & Lies*.

That's rather a lot of notoriety for one station but Holborn was back in the news in 2005 with a bizarre claim to fame – it is the most commonly mispronounced word in the English language.

The startling news emerged following a survey of 2,500 people to identify the words we struggle to get out correctly; Holborn emerged the winner, fending off stiff competition from such tongue-twisters as 'pharmaceutical', 'prescription' and, ironically, 'pronunciation'.

You are now of course wondering exactly how you do pronounce Holborn. The trick is to remember the 'l' is silent, which should spare you social embarrassment and impress your friends.

TUBE CARRIAGES IN THE SKY
2006

The shelf life of a London Underground carriage is limited. They cover hundreds of thousands of miles in their working lives, rumbling up and down the network, and when the relentless workload finally takes its toll, the faithful carriages are taken out of service.

For many, all the thanks they get is a final trip to the breaker's yard. Some escape that fate and are stored away out of public sight at one of Transport for London's cavernous depots but for the majority of the Tube's rolling stock, it's not a happy retirement.

But there are lucky ones. Some have found their way across the Solent to become part of the Isle of Wight's 'Island Line', while one carriage became an unlikely home to Radio Lollipop, the in-house radio station at Great Ormond Street Hospital.

And in 2006 four more unwanted carriages escaped the clutches of the crusher when they were snapped up by Village Underground, a charity supporting small companies, and turned into offices.

Nothing out of the ordinary there, you may think, but the location of the carriages-cum-offices has to be seen to be believed, perched precariously as they are on top of a viaduct in Shoreditch in East London with spectacular views of Canary Wharf and the Gherkin.

The idea was the brainchild of Village Underground's Tom Foxcroft, who was travelling on a train in Switzerland and idly realised that – without all the seats – his carriage would make a perfect office space. Back in London he pursued the project and persuaded TfL to sell him four old Jubilee Line carriages for the princely sum of £100.

It took him three years to get planning permission for their lofty location and cost £25,000 to winch the carriages into place. But once the seats had been removed and desks and lighting installed, the designers, independent record labels, script writers and photographers moved in.

'The idea came from my own experience as a designer trying to start a small practice with friends,' Foxcroft explained. 'We just couldn't get a foot on the ladder because of the price of studio and workspace, so I designed my own.

'The carriages are part of a much larger project to create a series of spaces in cities around the world to allow an international exchange of creativity and ideas. The essence of the project is that Village Underground will be a catalyst for new creativity.'

Foxcroft fought an early battle with local graffiti artists who would pay his carriages regular visits, but after tiring of the expense of jet-washing them clean he decided to embrace the offices' colourful urban decoration, reasoning that any tagger brave enough to climb all the way up the viaduct was nothing if not determined.

THE CADBURY CHOCOLATE
CONTRADICTION
2007

Underground commuters with a sweet tooth used to be able to happily indulge themselves on chocolate whenever they pleased, thanks to the proliferation of Cadbury vending machines that littered the network's platforms.

Sadly for London's chocoholics, Transport for London began to phase out the machines in 2007 and passengers must now locate what is known as a 'shop' in which to purchase their confectionery of choice.

But back in the halcyon days when commuters could simply pop their coins into a slot, the machines produced a puzzling statistic that no one has ever been able to explain, namely that the travelling public's most popular chocolate bar was Cadbury's Whole Nut.

The Whole Nut, of course, is a fine chocolate bar, an alluring combination of smooth, delicious chocolate contrasting with the piquant and crunchy nut. A really excellent treat indeed. The mystery is exactly how it managed to outsell its Cadbury's Dairy Milk stablemate, the best-selling chocolate bar in the UK, the crown jewel of the Cadbury range and the undisputed daddy of the choccy-bar racket.

Sales of Dairy Milk are estimated at a staggering £550 million per year worldwide but such figures apparently counted for little beneath the streets of London as commuters opted for the Whole Nut ahead of its more one-dimensional cousin.

The reasons for the gradual disappearance of the Cadbury machines are also something of a puzzler. Some say that a defective machine began pouring out smoke onto a platform and TfL decided they were a fire hazard, while others insist they fell victim to a deliberate campaign of decluttering the platforms in the build-up to the 2012 Olympic Games.

Whatever the truth, the myriad of newsagents with unfeasibly small booths on the Underground were all absolutely delighted.

DYNAMIC DON LETS HIS FEET DO THE TALKING

2008

The Tube is proud of its reputation as the best way to bypass London's inevitable traffic jams and get tourists and commuters alike from A to B without a chap needing a fresh shave by the time he reaches his destination.

But many years ago there was an attempt to embarrass the network in the speed stakes in the shape of the annual Beat The Tube race. Featuring a motley group dressed in pinstriped suits and braces, the race saw the competitors jump on a District Line train at Victoria heading for Wimbledon. At South Kensington they'd all jump off (minding the gap) and hotfoot it down 1.6 miles of the Fulham Road in an attempt to rejoin the same train at Fulham Broadway. They usually lost.

The Tube's pride, however, took something of a bashing back in 2008 when Olympic triathlete Tim Don was challenged to see whether he could outpace our beloved Underground on foot (above ground) in a couple of races.

The bookies' favourite was the Tube, with an average speed of 25mph compared to Don's more leisurely 15mph at full tilt, but sadly for the world's oldest underground rail network, it was David rather than Goliath's day.

The first challenge saw Don, the 2006 World Triathlon Champion no less, sprint the 965 metres between Baker Street and Edgware Road stations 4 minutes and 13 seconds faster than the train despatched on the Circle Line.

The rematch saw man and machine go head-to-head over 4,988 metres between Tower Hill and St James's Park and, although closer second time around, Don was again the winner by a single second.

'The Tube is a great transport system but if you want to get fit, you should give running to work a crack,' Don said, failing to conceal the smug grin on his face. 'I am really pleased. Exercise is essential and this shows it can be faster than commuting.'

The Underground immediately decided to give up drinking and takeaways and vowed to return fitter, stronger and faster the following year.

LOVE ON THE
NORTHERN LINE
2008

The Underground is not traditionally considered a hotbed for romance but according to a 2008 survey, the Tube is actually an aphrodisiac. The 'Tube Hottie' survey, carried out by social network website Qype, polled hundreds of commuters and some of the results were steamier than a Turkish bath.

'Forget "Misery Line" – the Northern Line should be dubbed the tunnel of love,' reported the *Metro* newspaper. 'In a result that will no doubt add to its overcrowding, the Tube line has been found to have the sexiest passengers.

'More than a third of people thought its combination of "spiky-haired indie kids" and "hot City types" gave it the edge over other lines. But there were major faults reported on the Hammersmith & City line – it had the least attractive passengers.

'Tube users spotted an average of four fanciable people every day, the survey found. Half admitted to having some sort of "Tube tryst", where they swapped numbers, dated or even had sex. But nine in ten admitted to a "missed moment" when they did not take things further with a fellow passenger.'

Saucy stuff indeed, and proof that overcrowding, body odour and intrusive iPods are not necessarily a barrier to finding love (or a one-night stand) on the Underground.

'The Tube has its own history, its own rules and its own etiquette,' said a Qype spokesman. 'Maybe that added romance of the whole Tube experience has something to do with the responses we got to our survey. You're not out at bars every day but you're always on the Tube so if you don't have a book to read, someone might catch your eye.'

Will Gull and Katie Crammer definitely caught each other's eye on the Underground in 2006 when they boarded a Central Line train for a journey that unexpectedly ended in them tying the knot.

The passionate pair got chatting after exchanging a couple of flirtatious notes and when the train pulled in at South Woodford Station and Will prepared to get off, they decided to go for a drink together. One thing led to another, Will subsequently got down on one knee and proposed on the platform at South Woodford in front of hundreds of passengers and they got hitched in 2011.

Mr and Mrs Gull were so taken with the romantic quality of South Woodford they even visited the station in full wedding outfits, but Katie drew the line at spending her honeymoon travelling on the Central Line.

'It is lovely to hear that we have brought this young couple together and that they have returned to South Woodford to let our staff know,' gushed a TfL spokesman, reaching for a tissue. 'We had more than 1.1 billion passengers on the Tube in 2010, so this can't be the only couple who have found love on the Underground and their journey ended happily in marriage.'

AN UNWELCOME HOLE
IN THE TROUSERS
2008

The average Tube carriage isn't always the cleanest of environments. The daily influx of millions of passengers means trains are prone to picking up all sorts of unwanted and unwelcome debris and detritus and in 2006 the *Evening Standard* newspaper reported a survey that discovered the average seat on public transport in London was home to more than 3 million bacteria.

An unsettling revelation indeed, but when one unfortunate commuter travelling on the Central Line in 2008 sat down to read his newspaper a few stray germs were the least of his worries.

Nothing initially seemed amiss but after a few minutes he noticed a burning sensation around his derrière and, starting to panic, he jumped off the train at Holland Park Station and alerted staff to his predicament.

An ambulance was called and police rushed to the scene to investigate the mysterious cause of the passenger's discomfort.

'We are not treating this as being malicious at this point,' said a spokeswoman for British Transport Police, who was obviously determined to get to the bottom of it. 'From our inquiries it seems that some sort of cleaning fluid has been spilled accidentally. The man was taken to Chelsea and Westminster Hospital suffering from skin irritation. There was some damage to his trousers.'

Whether his pride remained intact is another matter, but the unusual incident forced Transport for London to pull two trains out of service to ensure no more innocent trousers, not to mention passenger's bottoms, were harmed.

A TERRIBLE TICK-TOCK
2008

Delays on the Underground can be a major headache for commuters with unsympathetic bosses or passengers on a deadline, but even the most impatient of travellers could understand TfL's decision to suspend Hammersmith & City and District Line services through Bromley-by-Bow Station in the summer of 2008 when a bomb was uncovered nearby.

The unexploded Second World War ordnance was an absolute whopper and nervous police immediately set up a 200-metre exclusion zone around it, which meant the Tube couldn't safely stop at the station.

It was a wise move. As the brave boys of the bomb disposal unit got to work, the bomb started ticking and oozing an unidentified liquid, but once clean underwear had been sourced for the team they were able to stop the clock and make it safe.

'This is the largest Second World War bomb to be discovered in the past three decades,' said Chief Superintendent Simon O'Brien as he emerged nervously from his hiding place. 'It measures approximately the size and length of a man and weighs around 1,000kg. One of our hero colleagues from the Royal Engineers went back into that bomb four times, which is extremely unusual. I think he was very brave.'

Bomb scares are sadly a fact of life on the Underground, but in this case it really was a very scary bomb indeed.

The Underground's first experience of explosions actually dates all the way back to 1883 when Irish-American republican organisation Clan na Gael targeted the capital and the Tube in particular, blowing up part of a Metropolitan Line train with nitroglycerine and also damaging an engine in the tunnel between Charing Cross and Westminster.

Fortunately there were no fatalities as a result of the attacks and *The Times* the next day reported that it was 'greatly to the credit of the people of London that there has been no approach to panic, still less any rash impulses of suspicion and vengeance'.

The Home Secretary immediately drafted in 300 extra policeman in the wake of the attacks to guard the network but the 'dynamite wars' ultimately came to an end in 1886 as a result of internal divisions which weakened the dissidents and London commuters were able to breathe easily once again.

THE NAME'S BOND, UNDERGROUND BOND

2008

Devotees of James Bond will remember a scene in the 2002 instalment of the franchise, *Die Another Day*, when 007 (a.k.a. Pierce Brosnan) descends down a mysterious flight of stairs to Vauxhall Cross Station for a tête-à-tête with 'M' before picking up the keys to his new Aston Martin and embarking on another mission of derring-do, Martinis and impossibly attractive female spies.

Devotees of the London Underground will, of course, know that Vauxhall Cross doesn't actually exist but rumours persist that British Intelligence really did use the secret sections of the Tube at the height of the Cold War to avoid prying eyes and radioactive sushi.

Before MI6 moved to Vauxhall Cross in the 1990s, they were based on Westminster Bridge Road and the whispers have it there was a clandestine station on the network near Lambeth to ferry operatives to HQ throughout the 1960s and 1970s.

The powers-that-be have always refused to confirm or deny the rumours (and, to be fair, that's because it was their job to do so) but in 2008 it became crystal clear that MI6 *had*, in fact, had underground 'lodgings' during the war. This top-secret information came to light after a rather interesting piece of subterranean real estate was put up for sale. Though, of course, it probably wasn't advertised on Gumtree.

The property in question was a warren of tunnels under the streets of High Holborn. Previously subject to the Official Secrets Act, it emerged the tunnels had belonged to the enigmatically named 'Inter Services Research Bureau' just after the Second World War and were now up for grabs.

In fact, the 'Inter Services Research Bureau' was a research and redevelopment arm of MI6. Although the spooks had long since moved out to make way for the Post Office and then BT, it was proof positive that our finest spies really hadn't been averse to a spot of very deep cover.

TOO RUDE FOR THE TUBE
2008

Londoners are generally considered to be a cosmopolitan bunch who are not easily shocked but over the years that hasn't stopped the censor deciding what commuters should and should not be exposed to by way of advertising on the Underground.

Sparing everyone's blushes is a noble pursuit. No one wants their daily commute to be accompanied by graphic or explicit images and passengers certainly don't want to be forced into having the dreaded 'birds and bees' conversation with the kids as a result of a rather raunchy advert.

The censors, however, probably went a little too far in 2008 when they decided to ban a poster promoting an upcoming exhibition at the Royal Academy of Arts. The organisers' faux pas was to use an image of a 1532 work by German artist Lucas Cranach the Elder, which depicted Venus, the Roman goddess of love, wearing nothing but a smile. Actually she is wearing a fetching necklace in the painting but CBS Outdoor – the company charged with upholding moral values on London Underground advertising – were not for turning and the poster was pulled.

'We are disappointed and find it quite ridiculous in this day and age,' said a frustrated Academy spokeswoman. 'The painting is around 500 years old, it's a pure painting by a master.'

Hard cheese, responded TfL, insisting they couldn't care less about the artistic merits of Cranach's brushwork.

'Millions of people travel on the London Underground each day and they have no choice but to view whatever adverts are posted there,' a spokesman intoned. 'We have to take account of the full range of travellers and endeavour not to cause offence in the advertising we display.'

Venus is not the only poster to fall foul of CBS and TfL. In 2007 it was decided an image of a man breast-feeding a baby – an advert for online bingo – was deemed too unpalatable for the Tube masses, while in 2010 the authorities weren't happy with the image used to promote the latest album by popular beat combo Massive Attack, insisting the painting of a face looked too much like graffiti.

'They won't allow anything on the Tube that looks like "street art",' said the band's Robert del Naja, the man behind the image. 'They want us to remove all drips and fuzz from it so it doesn't look like it's been spray-painted, which is ridiculous. It's the most absurd censorship I've ever seen.'

It is easier to see why CBS has failed to green-light other advertising campaigns, particularly the 2005 poster for a TV series that featured Jerry Hall surrounded by a pack of half-naked men complete with dog collars and leads.

There was always going to be a furore when the makers of Rampant Rabbit, an adults-only item for ladies, tried to advertise on the Tube and, sure enough, CBS were quick to order the removal of all the offending items. To be fair, the artistic ad wasn't unduly graphic or rude but the danger that Aunt Edna might be subjected to such implied filth was just too big a risk to take.

CENTENARY CELEBRATION FOR ICONIC LOGO

2008

Brand awareness is vital for any successful business. It's all about instant product recognition, to borrow a dreadful management phrase, and if you've got an eye-catching corporate logo, the battle is already half won.

When it comes to business emblems, there are arguably none greater than the London Underground's iconic red circle and horizontal blue rectangle motif that can be seen outside every station and on every platform, proudly informing passengers exactly where they are on the network.

The world-famous logo is an example of what is called a roundel and its first version – a solid red disc and intersecting blue bar – appeared on the Underground back in 1908 to advertise the name of each station. Its distinctive but simple design helped passengers quickly distinguish it from commercial advertising and the logo proved an instant hit.

In 1913 Frank Pick, the Underground's publicity guru, commissioned a typographer called Edward Johnson to design a new typeface for the network and over the next few years the roundel was tweaked to accommodate the new lettering. The solid red disc became a circle as a result and once everyone was happy with the new design, it was registered as a trademark.

The roundel was a significant step towards giving the Underground a unified identify in a period when competing companies were still operating the different lines, and although the Metropolitan and District Lines both initially persisted with their own diamond version of the logo, they eventually saw sense and the roundel was here to stay.

Over the next two decades the roundel appeared on just about everything connected to the network, from stained-glass windows to steel masts, and today it is actually illegal to visit London without purchasing an overpriced coffee cup featuring the famous logo.

Since its introduction the roundel has spread like a plague beyond London and can now be seen outside cafés in Cornwall and shops in Slovakia. There is even a roundel on a sun shelter in the middle of the Black Rock Desert in Nevada.

The roundel celebrated its 100th birthday in 2008 and to celebrate the Art On The Underground group staged an exhibition to mark the milestone, inviting 100 artists to create a work inspired by the famous red circle and blue oblong.

Entitled *A Logo for London: 100 Years of Design Excellence*, the exhibition featured drawings, paintings, sculptures, collages and photographs from a host of the art world's big hitters, including Sir Peter Blake, Phillip Allen and Susan Hiller, and reached an even wider audience when the work was recreated in a series of posters on the network's stations.

'Nothing quite says London like the roundel,' said Moira Sinclair, Executive Director of Arts Council England. 'We are delighted to support this project with its 100 commissions to celebrate its 100th birthday.

'We hope that the work will help put art at the centre of London life and add an artistic treat to our daily commutes. We look forward to seeing these new posters reacting to one of the world's most recognisable, and best loved, icons.'

LEGAL EAGLE ON THE
WRONG SIDE OF THE LAW
2008

Complaining about delays on the Tube is something of a rite of passage for London's commuters, but it's prudent not to exaggerate the Underground's faults, as Erien Dubash discovered to her considerable cost after making a staggering 1,140 bogus claims for tardy trains between January 2004 and April 2007.

Dubash submitted a deluge of Customer Charter forms to Transport for London claiming refunds for delays on the Jubilee Line and, as a result, the solicitor was reimbursed to the tune of £3,885 for the inconvenience.

An embarrassment indeed for TfL, until one bright spark at the company realised that if each of Dubash's claims were really true, the Jubilee Line must have suffered significant problems every day for more than three years. A massive cross-checking exercise began to investigate whether they'd been duped.

They had, and at her trial at Southwark Crown Court in 2008, Dubash was finally found out. 'This defendant took advantage of the system by deception,' said prosecuting barrister Francis Sheridan. 'In consequence she submitted large numbers of fraudulent claims to obtain funds she was not entitled to.'

The judge wasn't impressed either, sentencing her to 200 hours of community service and ordering her to pay £8,000 in costs. Which all worked out a lot more expensive than buying a season ticket.

THE BIZARRE WORLD
OF THE LPO
2009

Commuters on London's public transport, including the Tube, are obviously a frightfully forgetful lot and the Lost Property Office (LPO) website tells us that a staggering 220,000 items per year are handed in to its HQ at the side of Baker Street Station, which works out at around 600 misplaced bits and bobs per day.

In 2009, the same year the LPO celebrated its 75th anniversary – and in lieu of a proper party with balloons and dancing and possible damage to the photocopier – they decided to open their doors to the public to reveal exactly what winds up in their cupboards.

The thousands of umbrellas, walking sticks and mobile phones cluttering up the shelves were no great surprise but things got interesting when the LPO admitted in the past passengers had also mislaid a lawnmower, a jar of bull's sperm, a stuffed puffer fish, a 14-foot boat and a suitcase stuffed with £10,000 in used notes.

'The amount of lost property handed in is going up every year,' said LPO manager Julie Haley. 'Nearly 200,000 items were handed in to the Lost Property Office [in 2008] and this is indeed a real testament to the honesty of Londoners. We do our best to reunite people with their property and would encourage anyone who loses something on public transport in London to get in touch with us.'

Two passengers who did just that were a scatterbrained university professor and an easily distracted medical courier.

The professor left two human skulls in a bag on the Tube, sparking a major police alert when they were discovered. It was only when the absent-minded academic came forward to explain the craniums were for educational purposes rather than the result of a grisly bloodbath that the boys in blue were stood down.

The courier in question was heading to a Harley Street clinic on the Circle Line with a package containing breast implants but, presumably transfixed by a fascinating advert for travel insurance, he got off the carriage without his cargo.

Turning up at the clinic, he realised his error, dashed to the LPO to retrieve his package and got back just in time to ensure the patient wasn't left feeling flat after her operation.

THE MOST BORING JOB
IN THE WORLD
2009

Keeping the London Underground looking its best is a mammoth task. The platforms, the ticket halls and the mile upon mile of tunnels all have to be maintained and the scale of the task when it comes to painting the network is on a par with the brushwork required to spruce up the Forth Bridge.

Transport for London, however, simply cannot shut down the system to let the decorators get to work. Passengers take a dim view of their next scheduled eastbound train being cancelled due to the application of a second coat of gloss, and TfL has a narrow two-hour window in the early hours of the morning to break out the rollers and stepladders.

Which is where Keith Jackson of paint manufacturer Aquatic Coatings comes in. TfL buys all its paint from the company and – believe it or not – Keith's job is to watch the paint dry and ensure it dehydrates in a timely and prompt fashion.

'It may be boring but it's important that the paint dries quickly,' Keith admitted in an interview in 2009. 'We make paint for the London Underground, which can only be painted between 3 a.m. and 5 a.m. Once paint is on the floor, it has to dry hard enough and fast enough for people to be able to walk on.'

Keith's typical working day sees him staring intently at a freshly painted wall, which must surely qualify as the world's most boring job. The highlight of his shift comes when he has to dab at the wall with a piece of card to assess the paint's consistency. He then clocks off and heads home for a quiet sob and an enormous drink.

'Customers want paint to dry quickly,' said Aquatic boss Anthony Kershaw. 'It is a crucial part of our marketing.'

So the next time you see a pristine, newly painted Underground platform, spare a thought for poor old Keith.

THE STATION IN THE SKY
2010

Many of the Underground's 270 stations are actually above ground but West Ashfield is unique when it comes to occupying an elevated position – it's actually three floors up in a tower block in west London.

To be strictly accurate, West Ashfield isn't a real station but Transport for London's state-of-the-art, £800,000 training facility where new staff are taught to deal with the trials and tribulations of the Tube, but it's so realistic you might be forgiven for thinking you had indeed discovered the network's long-lost 271st stop-off.

Opened in 2010, West Ashfield features a mocked-up platform (modelled on a westbound District Line platform) that can vibrate to replicate the arrival of a train, an Oyster card reader, a PA system, signal points and electricity power controls for that truly authentic Underground experience.

There's even a fan to simulate the blast of wind that accompanies a train when it emerges from a tunnel.

TfL now runs all manner of dastardly simulations at West Ashfield to ensure their staff can cope when they go out to work on the big, bad network for real.

'When you can make trains pile up to teach people how to respond, it's better than standing on a platform talking about it,' said TfL's Nigel Holness, somewhat ominously. 'We can also put on stressful situations to see how people respond in the control room. It used to be done by shadowing but now staff can learn by making mistakes that you wouldn't be able to make in a real station.'

UPSIDE DOWN AT WHITECHAPEL

2010

The London Underground has a fascinating relationship with its Overground cousin. The two networks usually cohabit in the capital peacefully enough but from time to time cooperation can give way to competition and the two sets of tracks have to be physically prised apart before anyone gets hurt.

The Underground and surface railway also frequently share stations in a marriage of convenience.

One such cohabiting arrangement is at Whitechapel Station, which was first opened to the public in 1876 when the East London Railway between Liverpool Street and destinations south of the River Thames was completed. It was remodelled in 1902 to accommodate the services of the Metropolitan District Railway and the Underground and Overground began more than a century of blissful coexistence.

The builders, however, were back in 2007 when the Overground section of the station was closed to allow work on the East London Line extension; the work was finally finished in 2010 and Tubes and mainline trains were running once again.

The new Whitechapel Station is strange, though. In particular, the location of the platforms is bewildering, with the District and Hammersmith & City Line platforms sited *above* the platforms for the East London Line Overground.

Or to put it another way, at Whitechapel the Overground is underground and the Underground is overground.

NO UNDERWEAR ON
THE UNDERGROUND
2010

One of the golden rules of travelling is to never, ever stare at your fellow passengers. Eye-contact on the Tube is strictly forbidden under any circumstances and the whole space-time continuum would be in mortal danger should commuters suddenly start eyeballing each other.

Saying that, there are a few exceptions and the stunned passengers who unashamedly gawped at four naked travellers in 2010 could definitely be forgiven for the temporary lapse in Tube etiquette.

The two men and two women were absolutely starkers and were it not for their handbags and briefcases to at least cover some of their modesty, it would have been even more embarrassing (and perhaps arousing) for all concerned.

The four stitchless passengers were not simply outrageous exhibitionists; they were actually part of a publicity stunt for a short-lived TV series called *The Naked Office* in which staff at struggling businesses were encouraged to disrobe in a bizarre attempt to turn around their company's fortunes.

'For most people in the UK going to work in the nude is a very daunting prospect,' said Steven Suphi, a behavioural expert with the programme. 'I believe this extreme process will help them push their boundaries and become a close team that trust each other enough to get naked together.'

Amazingly, naked commuting failed to catch on, which came as a huge relief to all the passengers who remained complete strangers to their local gym.

THE TOASTER THAT
NOBODY TURNED OFF
2010

Burning the toast is usually a minor inconvenience, warranting little more than a brief bout of mild swearing and another begrudging trip to the bread bin. We all make mistakes and until a loaf of Hovis costs £10, it's really not worth getting that upset about.

It's different, however, when it happens on the London Underground, and back in 2010 parts of the network were twice brought to a standstill after Tube employees accidentally decided to incinerate their favourite breakfast snack.

The two incidents both happened at King's Cross when staff popped their bread into the toaster, set the dial to 11 and then wandered off, only to realise the error of their ways when smoke began billowing out of the kitchen.

On both occasions firefighters had to be called and King's Cross was completely evacuated, much to the chagrin of the throng of seething commuters who were ordered to make their way to the surface until the offending toaster was located.

'This might sound minor but to shut such a busy station, which disrupts the journeys of thousands of passengers, is serious,' said the fabulously named Jo deBank of pressure group London TravelWatch. 'Perhaps there should be a toast ban across the network.'

A drastic solution certainly, and Transport for London immediately hit back.

'Staff have been reminded to take care when using the cooking facilities and we would like to apologise to customers for any inconvenience caused,' a TfL spokesman said. 'London Underground has extensive heat and smoke detection systems, fire alarms and sprinkler systems, and both alerts were dealt with quickly.'

Malicious toasters were not the only surreal cause of disruption to the Underground in 2010. When staff at Caledonian Road Station on the Piccadilly Line discovered smoke billowing from their mess room, they understandably feared the worst.

Close inspection by fire investigators uncovered an altogether more idiotic explanation.

'Upon inspection of room found the cause of smoke,' the official report tersely reported, 'someone had decided it was a good idea to store their box of Rice Krispies and four custard cream biscuits in the oven.'

Presumably the milk and tea bags were in the freezer.

THE FLASH MOBS WHO FLASH
2010

It's easy enough to forget your keys, mobile or wallet as you rush out of the front door, heading for the Underground and the daily commute to the office, but since 2010 scores of Londoners have been *deliberately* leaving their trousers at home for their journey to work.

The trouserless travellers are not clinically insane and they're not on their way to a knobbly knees competition.

They are in fact willing participants in what is known as the annual 'No Trousers Tube Ride', an unusual yearly occasion organised by practical jokers collective *Improv Everywhere*.

The event began in New York in 2001 and is now replicated on public transport systems across the world, in 60 different cities from Washington to Mexico City, Madrid to Toronto. Our American cousins naturally call it 'No Pants Day', but in London it has to be the 'No Trousers Tube Ride' in case anyone takes the US version too literally.

The aim is to 'have fun and entertain people', explained organiser Dan Becherano. 'The purpose of flash mobs is to show how we can get together without knowing each other and work as teams without really having seen each other ahead of time. The most important thing will be the victims – the reaction of people who aren't involved.'

Guidelines on the website for the New York event advised: 'You can wear fun underwear if you like but nothing that screams out "I wore this because I'm doing a silly stunt". Wear two pairs of underwear if it makes you feel more comfortable. Don't wear a thong or anything else that might offend people. Our aim is to make people laugh.'

Around 100 brave Londoners dared to partially disrobe for the first event in the capital in 2010, dividing into groups to travel on the network's different lines, and the number had grown to 150 by

2012 as word spread that showing fellow passengers your thighs was the in thing to do.

They certainly had more luck in 2012 than their counterparts in Madrid, who were stopped by the police before they could begin the challenge, proving that the Spanish aren't always as 'relaxed' about a flash of flesh as their reputation would have us believe.

Perhaps the most baffling fact about the whole thing is that it takes place in freezing January each year – which hasn't as yet dampened enthusiasm for the event.

THE GRAPES OF WRATH
2011

If you were brought up watching the antics of *Tom And Jerry* or any of the *Looney Tunes* on television, you're probably labouring under the misapprehension that when it comes to discarded fruit, a discarded banana skin poses the greatest danger to life and limb. Passengers on the London Underground, however, would be well advised to keep an eagle eye out for white grapes.

Whether seeded or their pipless cousins are the more hazardous is unknown but, according to official statistics, the aforementioned fruiting berry is definitely dangerous and should be avoided at all costs.

The number of accidents on the Tube is frankly staggering. A TfL database revealed that an eye-watering 18,677 accidents occurred on the network between January 2006 and March 2011. Thankfully only 188 proved to be fatal mishaps with the majority merely resulting in superficial injuries such as cuts and bruises.

'The safety of customers and staff is London Underground's top priority and a recent Office of Rail Regulation report indicated that the Tube is the safest significant-sized railway in Europe, with a safety record 15 times better than the European average,' reassured a spokesman.

'The latest figures show that safety incidents fell by 8 per cent in 2010–11 compared to the previous year. Although the vast majority of these incidents were very minor, and less than 0.0005 per cent of the five billion journeys made on the Tube in the last five years involved any kind of safety incident, we are not complacent and will continue to work hard to maintain our excellent and improving safety record.'

Which presumably means an imminent ban on the heinous hazard that is the white grape.

FOR SALE, DISUSED STATION –
ONE PREVIOUS OWNER
2011

It's a sad day when an Underground Station is closed down, consigned to the dustbin of transport history because it just isn't commercially viable. Some stations are cruelly left to rot when the doors are finally padlocked but for others, the end of their commuter days is merely the beginning of a new chapter.

Shoreditch Station was one of the earliest on the network, opening in 1869 as part of the East London Railway, but by the early 2000s the writing was on the wall with a meagre 1,130 passengers using its platforms each day. In June 2006 the axe finally fell and Shoreditch was no more, replaced by its upstart Overground counterpart Shoreditch High Street.

Initially the old girl seemed destined to fester and decay, forgotten by everyone, until Transport for London decided in 2011 to bolster its coffers and put the building up for auction.

'A single-storey building,' read the sales brochure. 'Previously Shoreditch Underground Station, the property compromises a ticket office, a lobby area, store rooms, plant rooms and a WC. The property is within a popular residential area with its many trendy bars and restaurants. Brick Lane is within easy walking distance and Old Spitalfields Market is close by.'

The spiel concluded with the reference 'public transport includes Shoreditch High Street Rail Station', which really was just rubbing salt into the wound.

The reserve price for the 1,688 square feet of building was £180,000 but when the former station finally went to auction in February 2011, she fetched an impressive £665,000. The new owners quickly got to work on the property and a few months after the sale, Shoreditch Station was reborn as an art gallery and events venue.

Other unwanted and unloved Tube stations have experienced contrasting fortunes since they were mothballed. The old Grade II listed ticket hall of Fulham Broadway is now home to an upmarket food emporium, while the long-forgotten South Kentish Town Station is now a *Cash Converters* shop with a pub next door, a happy coincidence for all those who need a drink after being forced to pawn their worldly goods.

BEWARE GREEDY
OYSTER CARDS
2011

Fans of the 1984 film *The Terminator* and its lacklustre sequels will be all too aware of the dangers of technology after the depiction of a malevolent computer system – Skynet – which becomes self-aware and (no doubt disenchanted with endless games of solitaire) attempts to wipe out its human masters with a nuclear strike.

At the time of writing, the Underground's Oyster card system has yet to try to obliterate London, but that's not to say the network's electronic ticketing scheme can always be trusted.

In fact, the next time you tap in or out at a London Underground station, be sure you're not getting ripped off. It turns out that in 2011 the Oyster card system had overcharged unsuspecting Tube, Overground and Docklands Light Railway commuters a staggering £64 million. That's more than a million pounds every week.

The eye-watering revelation came to light after a Freedom of Information request from Lib Dem London Assembly Group member Caroline Pidgeon, who was far from impressed by the pilfering machines.

'This level of overcharging is totally unacceptable,' she raged. 'There is something very seriously wrong when each and every week Londoners are ripped off by so much. Why has Boris Johnson, who has been chair of Transport for London, not taken this seriously in the last four years?

'Of course, in some cases passengers might forget to touch in and touch out, but such huge levels of overcharging clearly demonstrate that there are structural problems with how Oyster is operating. We know for a fact that at some stations, especially when the stations are very busy, maximum fares are automatically set for everyone passing through.

'It is time TfL stopped putting all the blame for Oyster overcharging on to passengers and started to recognise that they have a responsibility to ensure honest passengers are not ripped off.'

A Top 10 list was also published to name and shame the worst offending Underground stations in 2011. Ironically, it was Bank Station that was the naughtiest, overcharging passengers to the tune of £1,398,000 for the year, while King's Cross came in second with a figure of £1,126,000. Little old Leicester Square was 10th, electronically stealing a 'modest' £517,000 from commuters when their backs were turned.

God help us all if Skynet and Oyster ever join forces.

DARWIN DISCOVERED
AT LIVERPOOL STREET
2011

Although the Tube is a vital part of London's lucrative tourist trade, it isn't exactly a tourist attraction in its own right. The Underground gets visitors from Big Ben to Oxford Street but few tourists choose to spend their day admiring the network's subterranean splendour.

In 2010, however, Liverpool Street briefly enjoyed its moment in the spotlight when a waxwork of Charles Darwin unexpectedly made an appearance at the station, seemingly studying a map of the London Underground at the entrance to the Circle and Bakerloo Lines.

The life-size model of the legendary English naturalist drew big crowds but Transport for London were initially none the wiser where Darwin had come from until it transpired he had been 'kidnapped' from Madame Tussauds three days earlier.

The culprits were a self-styled guerrilla group called 'Free Charlie', who were apparently protesting at Darwin's treatment by Tussauds.

'The waxwork's hands were beginning to be coated with fine hair, its arms were lengthening and forehead getting larger, but Madame Tussauds refused to answer our concerns over faulty thermostats,' the group said. 'Either his waxwork is actually evolving, or it could be the work of creationists; nonetheless the old barnacle was glad to get away from [Albert] Einstein for a few hours.'

Darwin was promptly returned home after his unusual holiday and put under 24-hour guard while Liverpool Street reluctantly relinquished its temporary role as a public art installation.

IF YOU WANT TO BE A
RECORD BREAKER

2011

For most people speed isn't the essence of travelling on the Tube. Commuters like to get from A to B as quickly as possible, but with most Underground trains averaging a relatively sedate 20mph, no one is expecting to break the sound barrier on their way to work.

Speed, however, is exactly what it's all about for the intrepid souls who take on the long-running ad hoc competition known as 'The Tube Challenge', officially recognised by *The Guinness Book of World Records*, to see who can visit all the Underground stations on the network in the fastest possible time.

The rules of the challenge are simple. Competitors must visit every station on the network. They do not have to get off at each and every platform but the train must stop at the station. They are allowed to walk or use other forms of public transport to make connections between stations.

The trick, as you might imagine, is in the planning of your route. According to Marc Gawley, who set a new record for the challenge of 16 hours, 29 minutes and 57 seconds in 2011, there are six vital steps to success and by his own admission you have to be just that little bit obsessive in your preparation. It also helps if, like Marc, you are a fairly decent marathon runner.

'I run a management consultancy firm that specialises in solving business problems based on analytical approaches,' he said. 'I have a bit of an analytical problem-solving mind and could be considered something of a Microsoft Excel geek, so I needed to find a record where these skills came together with running long distances.

'I took my GCSE in Maths a year early, at A-level I studied Maths, Further Maths and Further Maths Additional and then went on to Oxford University to study Physics. Which, let's face it, is basically maths. So I'd probably be able to out-geek anyone on this. The Tube Challenge seemed perfect.'

Everyone politely agreed not to dwell on the fact Gawley hailed from Manchester and not London.

The first step in preparation is, unsurprisingly, the purchase of a good map. You then have to calculate journey times between stations, the frequency of the services on the different Tube lines and how long it takes to change trains at certain stations. Identifying stations you can reach on foot is also important before the sixth and most important step – generating your detailed final plan of attack.

The Tube Challenge was first staged in 1959 but the varying number of stations on the network over the years means the record time has fluctuated. Early competitors were also allowed to use cars and taxis to get between the stations, meaning their times were suspiciously quick – although with the current level of traffic on London's roads, it probably wouldn't help you much nowadays.

The challenge is not without its dangers, as Swedish pair Hakan Wolge and Lars Andersson discovered in 2006 when they set a new milestone.

'I had a close brush with doors closing around my knee with Lars onboard after a communication glitch between us,' Hakan said. 'After an eternity of me gesturing that I was stuck, the train driver finally conceded and reopened the doors. However she didn't start immediately but spent ten seconds giving me a verbal bashing over the speakers.'

Competition for the title of record holder is fierce and a little over a month after Gawley had registered his mark, serial challengers Andi James and Steve Wilson shaved 44 seconds off the record with their time of 16 hours, 29 minutes and 13 seconds.

At the time of going to print it was still the record, but in the cut-throat world of The Tube Challenge, things can quickly change – who knows, with a fair wind, a meticulously prepared spreadsheet and punctual trains, breaking the magical 16-hour mark could soon become a reality.

THE UNDERGROUND'S FURRY FRIENDS

2012

According to estimates, half a million mice have shunned their traditional pieds-à-terre in the holes of London's skirting boards and taken up residence in the Underground. Whether some unfortunate Tube employee has been tasked with actually counting the furry fellas or the figure is pure guesswork is unclear, but it's a big number. Approximately 1,850 little rodents for each of the Tube's 270 stations, in fact.

It would certainly require a lot of mouse traps if TfL ever seriously attempted to tackle the infestation.

Gnarled commuters are accustomed to seeing the little rodents scurrying around the platforms but it is of course far more entertaining watching tourists and out-of-towners jump when they first catch an unexpected glimpse of the furry interlopers.

The mice have also inspired a number of fictional stories about their subterranean adventures. The first was the animated series *Tube Mice*, which screened on ITV in 1988 and won an award for most imaginative title in the cartoon category later that year.

The second was *Underneath the Underground*, a 1996 book penned by former Blue Peter presenter Anthea Turner and her sister Wendy. Turner went on to write *How To Be The Perfect Housewife: Lessons in the Art of Modern Household Management* but most literary heavyweights believe her earlier Underground-inspired offering to be her most incisive work.

Such is the fame of the modern Underground mice that commuters at Farringdon in 2012 didn't smell a rat when they arrived at the station to be confronted with the following whiteboard message: 'The mice at this station have been attacking customers,' it read. 'Please place the bottom of your trousers into your socks to avoid being the victim of the Farringdon mice.'

Much tucking in and sartorial rearranging ensued and it wasn't until the following day that Transport for London confirmed the announcement was in fact a hoax perpetrated by a passenger with a rather dry sense of humour.

THE LONG AND
SHORT OF IT
2012

Thanks to Harry Beck and his user-friendly Tube map, a cursory glance at his Underground diagram suggests the distance between any two given stations on the network is pretty much the same. Regular commuters know that the truth is very different.

For example, the typical journey time between Leicester Square and Covent Garden on the Piccadilly Line is a mere 37 seconds, which frankly isn't even long enough to make any headway on *The Times* crossword. That makes the two stations the closest on the system and, were it not for the throngs of confused tourists on the streets above, it would be almost as quick to walk between them as it is to ride a carriage.

The journey time between Southwark and Waterloo on the Jubilee Line is also minimal at a rapid 41 seconds, while it takes just 42 seconds to travel between Charing Cross and Embankment on the Northern Line. Which is pretty damn quick.

In total, there are 14 trips you can make on the network that come in at under 60 seconds, with the jaunt between Shepherd's Bush Market to Goldhawk Road on the Circle Line the 'slowest' at an interminable 58 seconds.

At the other end of the scale, the longest average journey time on the Underground can be found on the Metropolitan Line between Chesham and Chalfont & Latimer, which takes 7 minutes and 20 seconds.

The tedious traipse from Wembley Park to Finchley Road, also on the Metropolitan Line, is 6 minutes and 50 seconds of your life you won't be getting back, while it's a full 5 minutes and 50 seconds to get from Hammersmith to Acton Town on the Piccadilly Line.

The Circle Line does not feature in the list of longest journeys but should you forget to get off the train, you could in theory be stuck on the same train for hours, going round and round central London without ever reaching your destination.

WATER, WATER, EVERYWHERE!

2012

The London Underground has always been prone to the odd flood but the network was hit by a deluge of biblical proportions in 2012 when 2 million litres of water flooded a section of the Central Line, causing hours of chaos to one of the busiest parts of the Tube.

The massive torrent left hundreds of damp passengers stranded before they were forced to make their escape on foot along the tunnels – and for once the inclement British weather was not to blame for the rush-hour disruption.

It was, it emerged, all the fault of a crew of heavy-handed workmen who had managed to crack a water pipe.

'We are usually to blame when things go wrong but this time we can put hand on heart and say, "It wasn't our fault, guv",' said a soggy spokesman for Transport for London. 'It was 100 per cent down to Thames Water. This has caused one of the biggest safety scares ever. There was so much water pumping in that there were genuine concerns of a tunnel collapse or the water flooding along the tunnel and affecting other lines.'

With the finger firmly pointed, TfL decided to call it a day, but Thames Water frantically tried to save face, claiming they were delighted the accident had happened.

'This has highlighted how weak the pipe was and the potential for it to burst at any time, so we are glad we can now get it replaced before the Olympics,' a spokesman said, desperately trying to keep a straight face.

'We're really sorry for the disruption that has been caused. We were doing exploratory work on the pipe in Wick Lane yesterday, having identified it as a potential weak point on the network ahead of the Olympics. This is a 24-inch pipe which is more than 100 years old and when we dug down to investigate a suspected leak, the earth around the pipe moved, causing it to burst.'

The shameless buck-shifting did little to improve the mood of the sodden commuters.

STICKY GUERILLA WARFARE
2012

It's a schoolboy error. You jump on the Tube for a long journey, only to realise you have failed to properly arm yourself with a newspaper, book, iPod or perhaps even some overdue crochet to pass the time, and you are now faced with a level of tedium on your journey that would break even the dullest of accountants.

The only solution is to read the Transport for London public service messages. You know, the ones that helpfully tell you you're rudely sitting in a priority seat or you can't get off at Tottenham Court Road because engineers are currently polishing the escalators. It's boring but it's better than staring at your shoes for 20 minutes.

In 2012, however, the messages suddenly got altogether more interesting as a craze for 'guerilla stickers' swept the Underground. Wags decided to replace the boring TfL missives with alternative pronouncements that weren't quite as serious.

'No eye contact – Penalty £200' was typical of the new series of subversive stickers, and 'We apologise for any incontinence caused during these engineering works' raised a few laughs. The warning that 'Peak hours may necessitate you let other people sit on your lap' had some passengers worried, while there were knowing smiles after commuters read, 'Please offer this seat to those drunks less able to stand than you'.

The maps in the carriages were not spared either. Oxford Street was renamed 'Nightmare On Elm Street' and Shepherd's Bush was rechristened 'Shepherd's Pie'. A spider's web even made an appearance inside the loop of the eastern extreme of the Central Line.

'It's a form of rebellion, whether it be due to the current climate of doom and gloom and people wanting to brighten their day,' a spokesman for the website selling some of the stickers told the BBC, insisting on anonymity in case TfL sent the heavies round.

'It's almost as though people are treating you as a drone and the signs are very serious. This is a bit of escapism and freedom that people can express relatively easily. I have seen more signs, more stickers and other designs, particularly based on the more common signs you see on the Underground.

'People can just take the sticker out, stick it off and be gone in a couple of seconds. But I'm not putting them up and the website cannot endorse them being stuck on the Tube.'

Not everyone was equally tickled by the rash of silly stickers. 'The costs of graffiti are substantial for the railway industry in terms of repairs and clean-up and can leave permanent scars on the infrastructure,' said a stern British Transport Police spokesman. 'It is a blight on our society and will not be tolerated.'

Reports that a subsequent TfL message warning 'Stickers are illegal – Offenders will be prosecuted' was replaced with 'Stickers are great – Keep it up' appear to be nothing more than rumours.

THE DANGERS OF
FALLING ASLEEP ON THE TUBE
2012

Grabbing 40 winks on the Underground after a hard day in the office or a few libations in a local hostelry can be extremely tempting. The Tube can be very soporific when you're tired and countless passengers have suffered the embarrassing experience of missing their stop after nodding off.

The repercussions of an impromptu nap, however, were nearly far more serious for Rakesh Nair in 2012 and almost led to divorce.

A chef on his way home late at night after a shift at an Indian restaurant in Westminster, Rakesh was minding his own business on a Jubilee Line train when a young woman sat down in the seat next to him and dozed off. Before he could say 'excuse me', the woman then leaned over and began inadvertently cuddling his arm, much to his obvious surprise and embarrassment.

On another day, the innocent incident would probably have been politely forgotten, but a fellow passenger had filmed the whole thing and uploaded the clip to YouTube, quickly attracting more than 500,000 hits from viewers who found the episode hilarious.

Unfortunately one of those hits came from Mrs Nair, who was definitely not amused. In fact, she was convinced the clip showed her husband *in flagrante* with his secret lover and went absolutely ballistic.

'I got into trouble with my wife, who thought it must be something quite serious,' Rakesh said. 'She didn't think it was funny to begin with. She thought it was a work colleague or someone I knew and started accusing me of these things.

'I said, "I didn't know the woman." She was convinced, eventually, and saw the funny side. All is well. Most people getting home at that time have been working and are obviously very tired, they don't quite know what's happening.'

The identity of the slumbering woman remained a mystery but the incident proved once again that you shouldn't believe everything you see on YouTube.

MICROPHONE MADNESS
2012

Spending hour after hour all on their own at the front of the train can do funny things to Tube drivers. Some mutter darkly to themselves, some sing and some can get very, very irritable by the end of an eight-hour shift during which absolutely nothing interesting or unusual has happened.

Others try to alleviate the inevitable boredom by livening up their frequent passenger announcements and for years the good folk at the *Going Underground* website have been collecting the funniest and most farcical for our enjoyment. Here are a dozen of the very finest, which require no further introduction ...

'I am the captain of your train and we will be departing shortly. We will be cruising at an altitude of approximately zero feet and our scheduled arrival time in Morden is 3:15 p.m. The temperature in Morden is approximately 15 degrees Celsius. Morden is in the same time zone as Mill Hill East, so there's no need to adjust your watches.'

'Beggars are operating on this train. Please do not encourage these professional beggars. If you have any spare change, please give it to a registered charity. Failing that, give it to me.'

'Welcome aboard the Flintstones railway. Once I get my feet on the floor and start running, we should be on our way.'

'Well, ladies and gentlemen, I can see a light in front of me which I think is probably Bank Station. So that's good, isn't it? I personally was hoping for Calais. Perhaps next time.'

'Please stand clear of the doors. Please note that the big slidy things are the doors.'

'Good evening, ladies and gents, and welcome to the Waterloo and City Line. Sights to observe on the journey are, to your right, black walls and, to your left, black walls. See the lovely black walls as we make our way to Waterloo. We will shortly be arriving at Waterloo, where this train will terminate. We would like to offer you a glass of champagne on arrival and you will notice the platform will be lined with lap dancers for your entertainment. Have a good weekend.'

'To the gentleman wearing the long grey coat trying to get on the second carriage, what part of "stand clear of the doors" don't you understand?'

'Come on, smile. It could be worse. You could be stuck on a plane being struck with deep vein thrombosis.'

'Sorry for the delay but there has been an incident at King's Cross. Someone has attacked the driver. The police have been called. It's a good thing I'm not a policeman because I'd lock them all up for life. Either that or shoot them.'

'Ladies and gentlemen, upon departing the train may I remind you to take your rubbish with you. Despite the fact that you are in something that is metal, fairly round, filthy and smells, this is a Tube train and not a bin on wheels.'

'Your delay this evening is caused by the line controller suffering from elbow and backside syndrome, not knowing his elbow from his backside. I'll let you know any further information as soon as I'm given any.'

'Ladies and gentlemen, I do apologise for the delay to your service. I know you're all dying to get home, unless of course, you happen to be married to my ex-wife, in which case you'll want to cross over to the westbound and go in the opposite direction.'

OLYMPIC CHAMPION KEEPS IT REAL
2012

The 2012 Olympics got everyone in London rather excited and to mark the big occasion the Olympic Flame took a little journey on the Underground from Wimbledon to Wimbledon Park on Day 67 of the relay, a trip that mercifully did not end in the train accidentally going up in flames, despite the obvious fire hazard.

A host of celebrities including rower James Cracknell, former Wimbledon champion Boris Becker, ex-England cricket captain Michael Vaughan and singer Katy B were on hand to add a touch of glamour to the day's proceedings and three days later the flame safely arrived in Stratford to signal the start of the Games.

The Underground, of course, did sterling work carrying thousands of fans around the capital during the Olympics, but one of the Tube's most heart-warming Games-related moments was completely unplanned and did not feature a single celeb.

It came in the wake of the final of the men's individual épée fencing competition. The winner was Venezuela's Rubén Dario Limardo Gascón, who clearly fancied celebrating his success, so after collecting his gold medal the South American decided to head into London to party.

He duly jumped onto the Docklands Light Railway – the result of a Tube cloning experiment gone horribly wrong – and then the Jubilee Line but, rather than hide behind a newspaper, Gascón was happy to pose for photos with his stunned fellow passengers and even allowed them to try his medal on for size.

'It was just amazing,' said one Olympic fan. 'This guy came on the train with a gold medal around his neck. I asked him about it and he just shrugged and said, "I'm a fencer from Venezuela."

He posed for pictures and signed autographs and then got off. It was absolutely surreal.'

Clearly no one had told Gascón that Underground etiquette usually demands absolutely no eye-contact and keeping your valuables out of sight.

UNDERGROUND FAILS TO LIVE UP TO ITS NAME

2012

Everything about the London Underground screams subterranean. The clue is in the name and when you consider the network was the first in the world to run a deep-level electric rail line back in 1890 and that Angel Station boasts a 60m-long escalator – the third longest in Western Europe – it's impossible not to get the impression we're talking below ground here.

But it's all an outrageous sham. A crass example of misleading marketing. A blatant attempt to pull the wool over our eyes.

The Tube's dark secret? More than half of the Tube's 249 miles of track are actually above ground. Shocking, isn't it?

To be fair, the Underground was far more faithful to its name in the early years, but as the network inexorably expanded out of the centre of the capital and into the suburban sprawl, space was at less of a premium and trains were able to run on the surface without fear of ploughing straight through a row of terraced houses or the local bus depot.

Today only 45 per cent of the track runs below the surface of London, with the rest winding its merry way in plain sight.

The longest continuous journey the modern passenger can make without seeing daylight is on the Northern Line between East Finchley and Morden Stations, a 17.3-mile trip (as long as they make the trip via the Bank branch rather than its shorter Charing Cross cousin). According to the Transport for London website, the journey takes an average of an hour, assuming of course there are no signal failures or passengers suddenly taken ill, giving the commuter a full 60 minutes of subterranean travel before eventually emerging into the light.

BOND BACK ON
THE UNDERGROUND
2012

Readers with a memory capable of spanning 40 pages or so will remember the Underground made a cameo appearance in 2002 James Bond blockbuster Die Another Day in the shape of the fictional Vauxhall Cross station.

Sadly the Tube failed to claim the Oscar that year for its gritty yet sympathetic portrayal of a sublevel MI6 stash of gadgets and gizmos, which may have had something to do with the fact the scene was actually shot on a sound stage at the famous Pinewood Studios in Buckinghamshire rather on the real network.

In 2012 Bond was back with a bang with the release of the critically-acclaimed Skyfall – the 23rd instalment of the franchise – and this time the Underground finally got to play itself on the big screen, charming audiences with a subtle but searing depiction of a subterranean public transport system on the edge.

The network's big moment comes as Bond chases baddie Raoul Silva after he escapes from MI6's clutches, pursuing him down into Temple Station, onto to a train and through Embankment before he finally emerges at Westminster for more flirting, fighting and, possibly, suit fitting.

The real exteriors of Temple and Westminster both make appearances in the film although the interior scenes were actually shot in a disused section of Charing Cross Station, which at least means the Underground was absolutely, definitely in the film this time.

The showpiece scene in which a train spectacularly falls through the ceiling of a Tube tunnel however was deemed far too dangerous to stage on the network itself and the producers headed back to Pinewood to recreate the big smash.

Which should hopefully provide reassurance for nervous tourists who struggle to separate fact and fiction and were worried that sort of thing happened on the network on a regular basis.

"The Tube train crash was one of the film's most complicated scenes," explained special effects supervisor Chris Corbould. "We couldn't use real Tube trains because they would be far too heavy, so we had to build our own in our workshop.

"Our carriages weigh about seven tons, whereas a real London Undergound train would be somewhere in the region of 20 tons. It took 25 guys, mostly engineers, about six months to make them. They had to be strong because we didn't want them to look fake once they crashed into the set.

"It's a spectacular shot and it worked perfectly. We could have done it again if we'd had to but it would have meant re-building a big part of the set, which would have taken a month or so. Fortunately, we didn't need to."

Skyfall was of course a big hit at the box office and buoyed by good reviews, the Underground went onto unsuccessfully audition for a part in Star Trek 2, proving how easy it is to become type cast in the movie business.

EVIL ESCALATOR THWARTS
'TIRED' BUSINESSMAN
2012

If legend – not to mention pages 50 and 51 of this very book – are to be believed, London Underground employed a one-legged stooge to ride up and down the network's first escalators in 1911, hoping public suspicion of the new-fangled contraptions would be allayed by the sight of their hired help effortlessly ascending and descending.

Tricky things escalators, you see. There are all sorts of potential pitfalls for the unsuspecting passenger, especially if they have perhaps indulged a little too lustily of the demon drink.

Proof positive was on hand in 2012 when an unfortunate Japanese businessman approached one such escalator at Tottenham Court Road Station and attempted to descend to the platform below, only to be thwarted by both machine and his own stupidity.

The problem was the chap in question decided to use an up rather than down escalator and every step he took in the vain hope of getting to a train proved completely futile as he was rapidly sent back to where he'd started.

Unluckily for the suited and booted businessman, his misjudgement and hilarious attempts to walk down the escalator were all captured on a camera by a fellow commuter, who was only too happy to talk to any media outlet that happened to be passing.

'I was making my way home after dinner when we quite literally bumped into this chap on the escalators between the Northern and Central lines at Tottenham Court Road station,' said Sam Napper, the man behind the camera. 'At first I thought he was playing silly buggers with a few of his mates but when we saw his dogged stagger and realised he was alone, I knew we were about to witness something truly brilliant.

'I had no idea where he came from but I had to hand it to him, the man knew where he was going. One by one, concerned commuters tried to steer him in the right direction, to no avail.'

The confused chap certainly looked like he might have had one too many drinks at the office party and for two whole minutes he fought the evil escalator. His ultimate victory was not falling over despite repeatedly inviting gravity to do its worse but he never did reach the platform and was eventually cajoled into turning around and forgetting about the whole sorry saga.

Modern life of course is never that simple and Mr Napper 'kindly' ensured the anonymous ambler would never be allowed to forget as incriminating footage of his subterranean silliness found its way onto the internet.

BIBLIOGRAPHY

Amazing & Extraordinary London Underground Facts, Stephen Halliday, David & Charles Limited, 2009

One Stop Short of Barking, Uncovering The London Underground, Mecca Ibrahim, New Holland Publishers, 2004

The Little Book of The London Underground, David Long, The History Press, 2009

What's In A Name? Cyril M. Harris, Capital History, 2001

Underground London, Stephen Smith, Abacus, 2004

A History Of London, Stephen Inwood, Macmillian, 1998

London Oddities, J E Hart, London Transport, 1974

Secret London, Andrew Duncan, New Holland, 2003

Guinness Book Of Rail Facts and Feats, John Marshall, Guinness Superlatives, 1971

The Penguin Guide To London, F. R. Banks, Penguin Books, 1973

ACKNOWLEDGEMENTS

During the writing of this book I found the following websites to be a ceaseless source of information, ideas and humour:

www.goingunderground.net
www.london-tubemap.com
www.londonreconnections.com
www.tubeplanner.com
www.abandonedstations.org.uk
www.randomlylondon.com
www.nickcooper.org.uk

Not forgetting ...

www.diamondgeezer.blogspot.com
www.ianvisits.co.uk

Also ...

www.districtdave.co.uk
www.metro.co.uk
www.bbc.co.uk

And of course ...

www.tfl.gov.uk

Many thanks must also go to Malcolm Croft and everyone at Portico Books.

THE STRANGEST SERIES

9781861052933

9781861055354

9781861052926

9781861051844

9781905798285

9781861059765

9781906032906

9781907554131

9781861054111

9781905798162

9781861057457

9781861056795

9781907554339

9781861059383

9781861058270